Published by Zodiac Publishing UK Ltd
65 Deans Street, Oakham, Rutland, LE15 6AF
United Kingdom
general@zodiacpublishing.org
www.zodiacpublishing.co.uk

First published February 2007
ISBN 978-1-904566-75-5

Text © Kimberly Saunders
Main cover photograph © John Nowell
Rear cover image © Graça Victoria - FOTOLIA and © tiloo - FOTOLIA
Design © Zodiac Publishing UK Ltd

Printed by TJ International Ltd

Budget Meals

*Eight Weeks of Delicious Dinner
& Dessert Recipes*

Kimberly Saunders

To Mom, who taught me everything I know about cooking, and to Fat Granny and Baby Granny, who taught me to love food.

Happiness is a good meal shared with those you love.

About the author

Kimberly Saunders was born in Atlanta, Georgia. Her father was a career enlisted Army man, so she grew up around the world on a budget. She comes from a long line of excellent cooks and many of these recipes are old family recipes. She enjoys cooking, baking, sewing on vintage machines and homeschooling.

Contents

INTRODUCTION

There is no need to think budget means cheap, low quality meals. It's entirely possible to create tasty, filling, nutritionally balanced but inexpensive meals. Some of what I say may seem controversial, but is not meant to offend.

The homemaker's first line of defence when attempting to hold down the food 'fort' is to make a plan of attack. This is the simplest bit of all. It's called a **meal plan**. A meal plan does not need to be restrictive. While I list my meals by day of the week, it's not unreasonable to move the meals about if you feel like having something different on a particular day. Usually, we find ourselves looking forward to meals when we know what we will be having, and how scrumptious it will be.

I don't think my kids will eat that

Don't fall into the trap of 'I don't think my kids will eat that.' Generally, children pick up subtle clues from the adults around them, and if they see a chink in your armour, or the slightest cue that there is a doubt, they will use it to their advantage by angling for 'junk food'. This is not so much about food, as it is a power struggle. Instead, involve your children in selecting the vegetables and preparing the meals, and let them taste, if possible, as they go along. If you have space in the garden, try growing some of your own vegetables. All you need to get started is a single square foot of ground, you can find loads of information about square foot gardening on the internet, and it is also a super cheap way to get organic vegetables! It is even cheaper if you join a seed exchange so that you don't end up with loads of unused seed, you simply swap whatever you have left over for seed you want. Children will take pride in their efforts, and a positive outlook will then act as a cue that the food is delicious and is a treat.

Some research shows that it takes an average of 18 experiences for the tongue and brain to identify a taste as being familiar and safe, so keep offering the foods, and get your children to at least taste it, don't substitute a different meal, and let time do its magic. Young children will not starve themselves, so if they don't eat, it's likely they are not overly hungry; this is not uncommon and goes in cycles. I know this will not be true of all children, but give it a proper try, and you might be pleasantly surprised!

If your child insists they're starving, try quietly placing the proffered meal before them once more and let it go at that. The child may try arguing, but don't let yourself be bullied into a worried position, nor an angry one. It simply means they are out to shift a sense of power, and by not giving in, you are sending a clear message. Genuinely hungry children will eat *something.*

How are you going to prepare your meals?

The second stage of attack, meal plan in hand, is know your method of cooking. What are the ingredients needed on your meal plan? From this comes stage 2 of the financial battle plan: the shopping list. Make a list of ALL the ingredients you will need. Do not leave a single item out, include sugar, salt, etc. You may know you have them on hand, but if you are using them regularly, they will soon need replenishing. Step 3 is to look at this complete must-have list and understand your weaponry: your supplies.

Look in the freezer. Look in the cupboards. Do you have any of the ingredients you need already? Are some of the items on the low side? If so, keep it on the 'to buy' list. If you have more than plenty of one item, you may simply cross it off. Do you have the appropriate tools to prepare the meals? Do you have a rolling pin, the correct cooking pan, and the proper utensils for that non-stick pan? No? Add whatever you need to your shopping list.

Where are you going to do your shopping?

You are now ready to do battle with the money hungry monsters who want to sell you stuff and make lots of money doing so - supermarkets! Armed with your shopping list, you now select your battleground. Look around, bargains can be had in surprising places. Go either early or late to supermarkets and grab marked down meat and vegetables. Farm shops and street markets are often cheaper than supermarkets, and frozen food offers excellent value. Tinned goods can sometimes meet your needs and have a long shelf-life, look for things such as mushrooms, peas and tomatoes. Go to your chosen ground and, this is the hard part, STICK TO YOUR LIST.

Buy one get one free

Those bargains are NOT a bargain unless it's on the list, and absolutely essential!!! Take advantage of voucher policies, and if supermarket shopping, look at the cost of frozen versus fresh, and do not hesitate to put things back if your last minute trolley check before the till says you need to. The aggravation of putting the item back versus saving a few pennies is well worth it, pennies quickly add up into pounds. You can further armour yourself by taking only a predetermined amount of cash with you, leaving cheque books and all cards at home and cutting a few corners as needed. Before you get to the till, go through your trolley. Did you put anything in the trolley that wasn't on your list? Take it out NOW. Did you pick up 3 because it saved a few pence, but you only really need one? Carefully weigh it up. If you won't use the extra in 3 weeks time, remove it. It's a common ploy to get people to buy more by offering 'deals', which upon closer inspection are not deals at all.

How to make a meal plan

The easiest way to start meal planning is to go through your freezer and cupboards right now, and make a list of EVERYTHING you have in there. Throw away any out of date goods, then look at what you have left and see how you can make them into meals. Create menus based around what you already have, and make a shopping list of the few things you need to buy to accomplish this. Keep the menu ideas simple, and avoid complicated recipes. You are doing family meals, not trying to run a five star restaurant. Also look at how you need to use your time, and plan meals around that. Out all day? Look at adding soups, stews and casseroles that can go in a slow cooker in the morning and be ready to eat as you walk through the door. Out for the evening? Try a meal that can be doubled easily, you can then freeze the extra and cook it from frozen for another meal. This can be anything from a simple homemade pizza, to meatloaf, mashed potatoes and vegetables.

If up until now you have been a 'just throw anything in the trolley and by end of the week the cupboards are totally bare' sort of person, you can still do meal plans. Make up 21 different meals, do a shopping list based on 7-14 meals or use the weekly plans provided in this book (depending on how you shop). Shop for the ingredients and away you go. Take note of things that are stock cupboard items and that you will tend to use week to week. Always make sure you have a spare of these items. Not five spares, just enough for a week should you ever need it.

I have included some simple meal plans to try, they have been successfully tested on my own family including my young children, and many of my friends have used them with great success with their own families. I have also included a short selection of favourite family recipes that can be substituted in case there is an allergy or a genuine dislike for a particular ingredient. Do remember, however, that sometimes a complete meal change is not necessary. My husband dislikes pasta and rice with passion, but we have substituted potatoes in everything from chicken rice roger (see page 48) to lasagne (see page 67), and it has been received with gusto. Simply look at the food type, in this case, a starch, and substitute accordingly.

But what about breakfast and lunch? And your snacks? Your food budget may fall down in this area without careful attention as well. These two meals are the most overlooked part of a food budget, and it's not uncommon for people to fool themselves about it. 'Oh, yes, we only spend £30 a week on food.' Really? Or do you spend £30 a week on most of your food, but buy lunch out and sneak breakfast from the corner shop? Fill up on biscuits from the vending machine? While this book provides the basis for your dinners and desserts, it is all FOOD and should come from the food budget! Plan these two other meals, and don't forget to add in snacks too. Planning these meals will not only save you money, but help you balance your diet properly. A balanced diet means you end up being properly fed, and you will feel fuller, and be less inclined to snack. This is as important for you as it is for growing children; it helps promote proper eating habits and a healthy lifestyle.

A good look at my sample dinner plans show that desserts are just fine, even within tight budget constraints, and can be good for you. They take up a slot in the daily dietary requirements by either being a bread group food, or by helping to provide some of the 5-7 servings a day fruit and vegetable requirement. This means that as part of your daily nutritional intake, you can eat these and know that your body will *use* the food you are eating, and less will be padded on as fat or waste. There is a balance between heavy desserts and the ones that are lighter in calories, so it all evens out. Keep in mind that your 5 a day means five *different* fruits and vegetables a day, so if you eat two apples, only one counts, so don't have apple Waldorf salad with lunch, and apple pie for dessert that night. Plan to have them on two different days.

It also goes without saying that taking your lunch with you is cheaper than buying it at a cafeteria or café, and most work places provide a microwave.

This makes it easy to take a good variety of lunches. Some leftovers are great cold, for example, cold fried chicken is very popular, and you can take a small pot of potato salad and a piece of fruit in an insulated lunch carrier. Likewise leftover meatloaf, mashed potatoes with gravy, and that spoonful of leftover peas can be carried to work and reheated in a microwave safe container. If a microwave is provided, there is no limit to what you can take. Save sandwiches for the days when you have no leftovers.

And on the subject of sandwiches, don't fall for false economy here. You can indeed buy very inexpensive loaves of bread from supermarkets, but be wary. They are typically full of sugar, puffed with air, and contain lots of preservatives. You can get decent bakery bread, but cheapest of all, you can bake your own bread without much effort. I know many people say it's *not* cheaper, but if you know what you're doing, it is.

You can bulk up your own bread by buying extra strong flour, using warm water, and 2 crushed vitamin c tablets, then following a recipe for a smaller 1½lb loaf, you end up with a nice 2lb size loaf. More bread at a fraction of the cost, and it's free of preservatives. This is true even if the loaf is made with half extra strong flour and half normal bread flour, half wholemeal flour, or even ¼ plain value four and ¼ normal bread flour. This is because yeast is active when it hits the warm water, and the vitamin c acts as a dough improver, enhancing the gluten so it reacts by rising higher. This makes it fluffy, but not full of empty air, and a bigger loaf means it goes further.

Now, about breakfast

You can make your own cereal bars, muffins for the week or have cereal. If having cereal, try varying it. Have cornflakes with sliced banana one week, hot porridge oats cooked in the microwave with sugar, cinnamon, and sultanas another week, or alternate between two of these in a single week. In winter if you want a hot breakfast, but get tired of porridge, don't forget eggs only take a moment to cook. You could have scrambled, fried or poached eggs. Semolina is a lovely cereal that can be eaten cooked like porridge oats, it makes a nice change, it's inexpensive and tastes great.

Snacks

We all get snacky from time to time. Plan for snacks! Get a quality cookie jar, one that is airtight so that cookies and biscuits will not go stale. Pick one day a week to do your baking and make your own biscuits. They are more nutritious and easier on the pocket. Do make sure you do your baking *after* you eat a good meal, so you don't end up stuffing yourself with a dozen chocolate chip cookies. And don't forget to eat your leftover puddings from dinner as a snack the following day, you are sure to have leftovers on some days so don't let them go to waste. Don't be put off by the act of baking. There's no secret except to follow the instructions and don't allow yourself to get distracted. If you have a super busy lifestyle, you may not have time to bake, in which case, I suggest looking at healthier biscuit options. Read the labels to understand what you are *really* getting, choose well, and remember, only eat snacks *after* you have had a good meal, and not within one hour of your next meal. Also make sure you are genuinely hungry, research has shown most people think their tummy is rumbly, and it's a jumbled up signal for mild thirst. So if you do not drink much fluid, or drink lots of tea and coffee, have water, milk, or juice first, wait ten minutes, and then see if your stomach still roars.

Done together and with commitment, your meal planning can assist you to feed a family well on a surprisingly low budget.

Plan your meals
Check those cupboards
Stick to your shopping list
Look for discounted foods and cheaper brands
Drink plenty of fluids
Be cheerful about eating
Eat food from home
SAVE CASH!

Getting started

- Recipes serve four people, unless mentioned.
- Measurements are given in cups or fluid ounces so you don't need to use scales, only measuring cups and spoons.
- Add extra vegetables as a side dish - I've left this part up to you so use seasonal vegetables or just whatever you've got in the freezer.

Basic pastry & bases

Here are the basic recipes for bases and pastry used throughout this book.

Filo dough

22 oz plain flour	1 tsp salt
4 oz warm water	2 tbsp vegetable oil

Mix flour and salt together in a bowl. Gradually add the water, stirring to make a stiff dough. Turn onto a pastry board. Place the oil in a bowl and spread a little of it on the palms of your hands. Knead the dough adding more oil to your hands when it becomes sticky. Continue until you have a smooth, elastic ball of dough and the oil is nearly all gone. Then roll the ball in the oil to cover all sides. Separate ¼ of the dough and roll to ¼ inch thickness on a board rubbed with cornstarch. Cover with a clean cloth and let it rest for 10 minutes. Cover a table (card table or larger) with a smooth cloth and carefully lift dough onto it. Put your hands under the dough, palms down, and gently stretch dough with the backs of your hands, working your way around the table, until dough is as thin as tissue paper. Don't worry if it hangs down around the edges. Cut off the thicker edge and save the scraps. They can be put in a moist bowl, kneaded and rolled again. The Filo is now ready to be cut in pieces with scissors if you wish to use it moist. If you prefer dry Filo, allow it to stand for about 10 minutes, then cut into desired size.

Hints on handling Filo
Use moist, not dry, sheets of Filo, with moist mixtures (cheese, custard, meat or vegetable fillings). Always use moist Filo in a recipe in which the Filo is rolled or folded. Dry Filo can be sprinkled or brushed with water to make it more pliable. The sheets of Filo dry quickly so keep all but the sheet you are working with covered with a towel. Don't unwrap until you have the filling prepared and are ready to use it.

Baked homemade digestives

Quantities are whatever you like. The ratio is 1 = 100g or 4oz, enough for a good plateful of biscuits.

1: oatmeal   1: wholemeal flour
1: butter   ½: caster sugar

Mix all the ingredients together like pastry (rub in the butter with your fingers). Add a tiny bit of cold water to help it stick together. Roll out thinly (3mm, ¼in). Use a round cutter to make circles and place on a baking tray. Bake for 15 minutes in a hottish oven (200°C or so) - make sure they don't go dark brown! Cool on a wire rack.

Tortillas for tacos

8 oz flour   4 oz polenta (cornmeal)
¼ tsp salt   1 egg
12 oz cold water

Combine all ingredients in a bowl and beat until smooth. The batter will be thin. Spoon 3 tbsp of batter on a moderately hot ungreased frying pan to make a very thin 6 inch pancake. Turn when edges begin to look dry, but not brown. Fold shells in half and fasten with toothpick or skewer. Put 2 or 3 shells in a skillet of hot oil. Cook on both sides for just a few seconds. Remove and drain on brown paper. Fill as you normally would for tacos, see page 47 for other ideas.

Short crust pastry

8in, 9in or 10in single crust

11 oz plain flour	½ level tsp salt
4 oz butter (or margarine)	3 tbsp ice cold water

8in or 9in double crust

16 oz plain flour	1 level tsp salt
6 oz butter (or margarine)	5 tbsp ice cold water

9in deep dish double crust or 10in double crust

22 oz plain flour	1 tsp salt
8 oz butter (or margarine)	7-8 tbsp ice cold water

Combine flour and salt in a medium sized mixing bowl. Cut in butter using 2 knives until all flour is blended in to form pea-size chunks. You do this by cutting the butter into tiny pieces and mixing it in slowly. Sprinkle in water, one tbsp at a time. Toss lightly with a fork just until the dough will form balls. Divide dough in half, if making double crust. Press between hands to form one or two 5-6in pancakes. Flour dough lightly. Roll into a circle, slightly larger than desired. Then fold dough carefully into quarters and place in to your pie dish. Then unfold and press into the pie plate. Press gently into the plate to fit, and fold the edge over gently under the edge and flue edge.

For double crust pie, trim to fit the edge, fill with desired filling, then place the top crust on. Press edges together with a fork to seal and trim edges. Cut a few slits in the top to allow it to vent.

Sweet scones

16 oz self raising flour   3 tsp baking powder
2 tbsp sugar   4 oz plus 2 tbsp milk
3 oz vegetable oil

Mix flour, baking powder and sugar in a bowl. Add milk and oil; stir just enough to hold the dough together. Knead lightly (about 10 strokes) on a well-floured surface. Pat or roll dough about ½in thick (makes about a 7in circle) and cut with a floured cutter. Place on an ungreased cookie sheet. Bake at 220°C in a preheated oven for 10-12 minutes, until golden brown.

For a savoury scone base, omit the sugar, keeping the other ingredients the same.

Week 1

Shopping List

1 small lettuce
2 tomatoes
1 cucumber
4 small onions
bag of potatoes
3 leeks
1 red bell pepper (capiscum)
1 orange
2 red apples
grapes, seedless
cherries

cheddar cheese
milk
margarine
butter
plain yoghurt
eggs
6 oz cottage cheese
2 lard or vegetables lard (such as pura)

1 jar cranberry sauce
green beans, frozen or tinned
1 tin salmon or tuna
1 tin pink salmon
1 12oz tin sweet corn
petit pois (peas), frozen or tinned
1 tin mushy peas
1 tin fruit cocktail
1 tin peaches in syrup
1 tin strawberries in syrup
1 tin raspberries in syrup
1 tin pineapple chunks

4 pork steaks
1 small chicken
sausages
4 fish fillets, undyed
pork roast

bag of long grain rice
bag of dried pasta

vinegar
BBQ sauce
black pepper
salt
vegetable stock cubes
vegetable oil
curry powder
dried parsley
dried mixed herbs
garlic powder

lemon juice
1 tin evaporated milk
vanilla essence
unflavoured gelatine
cinnamon
nutmeg
yeast
sugar
bread crumbs
granola cereal
plain flour
self raising flour
icing sugar

apple juice

Sunday

Roast pork with leek

1 pork roast   3 leeks
garlic powder   4 oz water

Preheat oven to 240°C. Place all the ingredients in a roaster and cook for
30 minutes. Then reduce the temperature of the oven to 190°C and cook
for a further 30 minutes for each 500g plus an additional 30 minutes. Baste
the roast with its juices every 20 minutes.

Slow cooker method
Cut up leeks and place some in bottom of your slow cooker. Rub roast
lightly with garlic powder. Place roast on top and cover with remaining
leek. Add 4 oz water. Cook on high for 6 hours or on low for 9-10 hours.

Strawberry whip

1 tin strawberries in syrup
1 envelope unflavoured gelatine
1 tin evaporated milk (or milk substitute)

Drain syrup from strawberries into a microwave-safe jug and sprinkle the
gelatine over the liquid. Allow to soften for 5 minutes, then stir well until
dissolved. Heat on high in microwave for 90 seconds. Allow to stand 1
minute, then remove and stir well. Top up the liquid amount with the
evaporated milk (or milk substitute) to make up one pint. In a mixing
bowl, puree the strawberries and pour the gelatine liquid over and whip
until frothy and well mixed. Using a soup ladle, spoon into a dessert bowl
and place in the bottom of the refrigerator towards the rear of the shelf for
at least an hour.

Monday

Cranberry pork steaks

4 pork steaks	½ jar cranberry sauce
4 oz BBQ sauce	4 oz water
4 tbsp plain flour	black pepper, to taste

In a frying pan, brown the pork steaks, seasoning lightly with black pepper. Drain off excess fat, and in a measuring jug, combine cranberry sauce, BBQ sauce, and water. Pour this over the pork steaks. Cover and simmer on low for 45 minutes. Remove the chops and cover with a clean tea towel to keep warm. In the measuring jug, whisk 2 oz water and 4 tbsp plain flour, then stir into the sauce in the pan. Cook until thickened and bubbling. Serve on top of rice and spoon sauce over the chops.

Cinnamon swirl loaf

28 oz plain flour	1 package active dry yeast
1 oz water	1 tsp salt
1 cup milk	2 eggs
2 oz sugar	3 oz sugar
2 oz lard	1 tbsp cinnamon

Preheat oven to 200°C. In a large mixing bowl, combine half the flour and the yeast. In a small saucepan, heat together the milk, water, lard, 2 oz sugar and salt until warm (about temp of warmed baby milk), stirring occasionally to melt the lard. Add to the flour and yeast, and then add the eggs. Beat for three minutes at high speed, then add the remaining flour.

Lightly flour a board or clean counter, and lightly knead dough until it's smooth then place in a large lightly oiled bowl, turning once so all sides are oiled. Cover and place in a warm place (such as an airing cupboard) and let rise for 2 hours. Punch down then roll out to a 15in x 7in rectangle, about ½in thick.

Mix 3 oz sugar and the cinnamon, and sprinkle over the rectangle. Roll up Swiss roll style, starting with the narrow end. Seal the long edge, and place in a lightly oiled pan. Cover and let rise for 1 hour. Bake for 40 minutes. When cool, drizzle with icing sugar glaze, the recipe is given below. Great warmed or sliced for toast for breakfast.

Glaze

1 tbsp milk   8 oz icing sugar
½ tsp vanilla

Mix the ingredients together and drizzle over the loaf.

If you are using a bread maker, simply add the ingredients in the usual order recommended by your maker. Bake on setting for fruit loaf, and then drizzle the glaze over the loaf when done.

Tuesday

Chicken cheese bake

1 small chicken, cut up	2 oz plain flour
3 oz vegetable oil	4 oz milk
4 oz cheddar cheese, grated	1 onion, diced
1 vegetable stock cube	black pepper, to taste

Coat the chicken in plain flour then brown in the oil. Place the chicken in a casserole dish. In a pan, crumble up the stock cube and add the milk, cheese and onion, and 2 tbsp of the leftover flour. Heat and stir until cube is dissolved and the cheese melted, and pour over the chicken. Lightly pepper the top with black pepper and bake in preheated 200°C oven for 1 hour.

Yoghurt parfait

plain natural yoghurt	1 tsp vanilla
icing sugar	granola cereal

Take the plain natural yoghurt and sweeten by stirring in icing sugar and vanilla. Add the sugar by the tablespoon until sweetened to your taste. Take serving containers and fill ¼ way with granola cereal. And top with an equal amount of sweetened yoghurt, then layer again with granola and top with more yoghurt.

Wednesday

Salmon patties

1 tin of salmon (or tuna)   1 egg, beaten
4 oz plain flour   1 small onion, diced

Lightly drain fish, mix with beaten egg, flour and diced onion. Form into patties and shallow fry in a pan. Drain the cooked patties on clean kitchen roll or reserved clean j cloths.

Corn fritters

1 egg   8 oz self raising flour
4 oz milk   1 tbsp vegetable oil
1 12 oz can sweet corn

Beat the egg and milk together then mix in the sweet corn and the oil. Stir in the flour just enough to mix, and drop by tablespoons into hot frying oil in a frying pan. Drain on kitchen roll.

Tomato salad

lettuce   cucumber
tomatoes   3oz cheddar cheese

Shred lettuce, slice the cucumber and the tomatoes, cube the cheddar cheese, and toss together with vinaigrette dressing.

Dressing
4 oz vegetable oil   1 tsp mixed herbs
2 oz vinegar   1 tsp garlic powder
2 tbsp water

Combine all the ingredients in a bottle and shake well until mixed, then pour immediately. If it separates, simply shake again before using.

Wednesday - continued

Peach pie

Pastry for a two crust pie (page 14)   1 tin peaches in syrup
2 tbsp margarine   ½ tsp cinnamon
2 tbsp plain flour

Roll out the pastry and line a pie tin. Place peach slices in the bottom. In a small sauce pan, place the syrup from the peaches and cinnamon, then stir in the flour. Cook over medium low heat until thickened, then pour over the peaches, and top with the second crust and seal edges. Cut 4 vents into the top, and bake in centre of preheated 220°C oven for 40 minutes.

Plan one day a week to prepare things like pie crusts. This is a great make ahead pie if you're baking once a week.

Thursday

Cheesy potatoes and sausages

8 sausages	½ onion, chopped
2 oz plain flour	16 oz milk
4 oz cheese, grated	24 oz potatoes, sliced

In a frying pan, cook the sausages, then place on a plate and slice lengthwise. Brown the onion, stir in the flour, adding the milk and cook until thickened. Remove from heat, and stir in the cheese. Lightly oil a casserole dish, and layer with half of the potatoes, then with sausages, then top with the cheese sauce, and repeat. Bake in centre of preheated 200°C oven for 1 hour 15 minutes.

You can spice this meal up by adding 1 tbsp sandwich mustard, or a dash of Worcester sauce, or adding garlic, herbs, and black pepper.

Serves 6.

Spice cake

6 oz margarine	6 oz sugar
3 eggs	6 oz self raising flour
½ tsp nutmeg	1 tsp cinnamon

Beat the margarine and sugar until very creamy, then beat in eggs one at a time. Add in the flour and spices, slowly, and then whip until light and airy. Place in two round cake tins, and bake in centre of a preheated 200°C oven for 20 minutes. When cooled, make some of the icing glaze as before for the cinnamon loaf (page 21), and drizzle between the layers and on top.

Friday

Fried fish

2 oz plain flour   1 egg
4 fish fillets   breadcrumbs
1 tbsp vegetable oil

Place plain flour in a bowl. In a separate bowl, beat the egg with 1 tbsp of flour. Take your 4 fish fillets and lightly coat with flour, then dip in the egg mixture, and roll in breadcrumbs. Heat vegetable oil in a frying pan and fry in hot oil on both sides, about 10 minutes each side, until fish is tender and golden. Drain on kitchen roll. Serves 4-6 depending on size of fillets.

Fruit salad

16 oz apple juice   1 tbsp lemon juice
½ tsp orange zest, grated   2 tsp ground cinnamon
2 red apples, cored and chopped   12 oz pineapple chunks
1 orange, peeled and sectioned   4 oz seedless grapes
2 oz cherries, pitted and sliced

In a medium saucepan, combine apple juice, lemon juice, zest and cinnamon. Heat to boil and simmer uncovered for 10 minutes. Cool to room temperature.

In a large serving bowl, combine apples, pineapple, orange, cherries and grapes. Pour juice mixture over fruit. Chill before serving.

Serve with cream or ice-cream, if desired.

Saturday

Salmon kedgeree

1 medium onion, finely chopped	1 tbsp garlic powder
1 tsp curry powder	6 oz long grain rice
1 red pepper, sliced and seeds removed	
1 vegetable stock cube (dissolved in 8 oz boiling water)	
1 tin pink salmon	4 hard-boiled eggs, quartered
2 tbsp dried parsley	black pepper, to taste

Heat some vegetable oil in a frying pan and gently fry the onion for a few minutes until it softens. Add the garlic and curry powder. Cook for one minute. Add the rice, capsicum and vegetable stock to the pan.

Bring to the boil and then simmer, covered, for 12 minutes or until the rice is cooked. Add the salmon and eggs and gently fold them through the mixture. Stir in the parsley and add pepper to taste.

Raspberry mousse

1 tin raspberries in syrup	6 oz cottage cheese
1 tsp vanilla essence	

Drain the syrup from the raspberries into a measuring jug, reserving 3 oz of the liquid. In a mixing bowl, place the cottage cheese and raspberries and puree. Add the reserved syrup and vanilla and whip. It should be the consistency of softened ice cream. Place into dishes and serve.

Week 2

Shopping List

large bag of potatoes
4 small onions
4 mushrooms sliced (or 1 tin sliced mushrooms)
carrots
1 bag of eating apples

eggs
large container natural yoghurt
butter/margarine
pint whipping cream
1 carton orange juice
milk

tin of strawberries
tin of sliced peaches
tin of black eyed peas
bottle of lemon juice

1 large chicken
1 bag mixed chicken parts or drumsticks, or chicken breasts
sausages
750 g mince
4 pork steaks

bag of value rice

box of super cook gelatine
cinnamon
vanilla essence
plain flour
self raising flour
ground nutmeg
sugar
porridge oats
jar of value mixed fruit jam
bag of value sultanas
1 tin evapourated milk (optional)

BBQ sauce
vegetable stock cubes
chicken stock cubes
beef stock cubes
garlic powder
mixed dried herbs
vegetable oil

bag of frozen green beans
bag of frozen peas

Sunday

Roast chicken dinner

1 chicken	8 medium potatoes
1 bag peas, frozen	2 tbsp flour
4 oz water	1 onion, diced
1 chicken stock cube	

Roast the chicken according to package direction with the potatoes. Gently cook the peas shortly before chicken and potatoes are done. Gently cook the onion. To make the gravy, put 2 tbsp flour in a pan and whisk with 4 oz water till smooth, then crumble in ½ stock cube and add boiling water to make ½ pint liquid. Whisk well, add onion, and heat on low until it's the right consistency.

Lancashire apple cake

3 eggs	4 oz orange juice
12 oz sugar	4 oz vegetable oil
24 oz self raising flour	1 tsp vanilla essence
1 tsp cinnamon	24 oz apples, chopped
½ tsp nutmeg	

Preheat oven to 200°C. Lightly grease a cake tin. In a bowl, beat the eggs until frothy. Add the sugar and mix well, then stir in all the dry ingredients. Stir in orange juice, oil, and vanilla. The batter will be thick, so you will need to fold in the chopped apples to ensure they are evenly distributed. Spoon mixture into tin and bake for 50-60 minutes.Cool on a wire rack for 15 minutes and then carefully turn cake out.

Homemade custard

1 pint milk	1 tsp vanilla essence
2 tbsp plain flour	

Whisk ½ milk with the flour in a pan, top up with rest of milk, and heat over a medium low heat till thickened to desired consistency. Remove from heat and add vanilla.

Monday

Meatloaf

500 g mince

1 sliced mushroom

1 tsp garlic powder

1 egg, beaten

2 additional tbsp BBQ sauce

½ small onion, diced

2 tbsp BBQ sauce

2 tsp mixed dried herbs

3 oz porridge oats

Preheat oven to 200°C. In a bowl, place mince and all other ingredients except one of the 2 tbsp BBQ sauce. Mix together very well. This is also easily done with a mixer or food processor (food processor with plastic blade in, mince can still be frozen though). Place into ungreased loaf pan and spoon over remaining 2 tbsp BBQ sauce over the top. Bake for 25 minutes.

Mixed fruit yoghurt

1 large container plain yoghurt

1 tbsp mixed jam

4 tsp sugar

1 tsp vanilla essence

If you make homemade yoghurt, make up a batch of yoghurt, adding in 1 tsp sugar and a tablespoon of mixed fruit jam. If not, buy a *large* container of plain live yoghurt. Measure out 6 oz for each person into a liquidiser or food processor with mixing blade on; add 1 tsp of sugar per person, and 1 large tbsp of mixed jam, and a single tsp vanilla essence. Whiz on high for a minute or two till thoroughly mixed, taste to check it is sweet enough, then spoon into bowls or serving cups and refrigerate.

Tuesday

BBQ chicken

1 piece of chicken per person   BBQ sauce

Preheat oven to 220°C. Cook chicken for 30 minutes then coat with the BBQ sauce, and place under the grill for additional 10-15 minutes.

Slow cooker method
Coat chicken with BBQ sauce and cook on low for 6 hours if chicken is boneless or 7 if on bone.

Serve with mashed potatoes and gravy (see below for the recipe).

Gravy
½ chicken stock cube   2 tbsp plain flour
½ pint water

Use enough water to whisk the flour into a smooth paste, then add remaining water and bring to the boil, stirring all the while. Then whisk until smooth.

Peach cobbler

1 sweet scone base (see page 15)   1 tin peaches
butter

Make a sweet scone base, adding just enough juice or syrup from the peaches to make the scone mix runny. Drain the rest of the juice from the peaches (save for smoothies). Place peaches in a baking tin, and pour scone batter over the top. Dot with butter. Bake at 200°C for 20 minutes, or until a knife comes out clean from the batter topping. Cobbler will be moist so there's no need for custard or cream.

Wednesday

Pork steak & garlic potatoes

4 pork steaks	4 potatoes, peeled and diced
garlic powder	green beans

Cook pork steaks according to package directions (about 30 minutes in oven at 200°C, if defrosted) after dusting lightly with the garlic powder. Boil the potatoes and season with garlic and butter to taste.

Slow cooker method
Place potatoes in steamer basket or bottom of slow cooker. Lightly dust with garlic powder if slow cooker, add just barely enough water to cover the potatoes. Next basket or on top of potatoes in slow cooker, place the pork steaks, having *lightly* salted and peppered them. Next, layer the green beans. Cook till meat is done in steamer and potatoes tender, in slow cooker this will be 6 hours on low.

Great for slow cooker or steamer!

Natural orange jelly

1 envelope plain gelatine	9 oz boiling water
9 oz orange juice	3 oz sugar

Pour boiling water into glass measuring jug and IMMEDIATELY, sprinkle the sachet of gelatine over the water (never do this the other way round, it makes a horrific unusable mess). Stir briskly till dissolved, and then stir in sugar, and lastly the orange juice. Pour into serving dishes and chill till set (about 1-2 hours).

No artificial colours, no artificial flavourings, no sweeteners, and counts towards the 5 a day. Also cheaper than even value brand jelly!

Thursday

Lemon chicken

chicken pieces, frozen	lemon juice
8 oz rice	mushrooms, sliced
½ onion, diced	16 oz water
1 chicken stock cube	

Place the frozen chicken pieces in a large dish. Pour enough lemon juice in to marinate the breasts as they defrost. Leave in fridge to defrost, for at least 1 hour (it is okay if not completely defrosted.) Chicken will whiten in places, this a natural bleaching action of the lemon juice!
Preheat oven to 200°C. Place rice in a casserole dish, stir in mushrooms and onion. Dissolve the stock cube in the boiling water and pour it over the rice. Place chicken breasts on top and pour over remaining lemon juice marinade. Bake for 1 hour.

Strawberry trifle

4 sweet scones (see recipe page 15)	9 oz water
1 packet unflavoured gelatine	1 tin strawberries in juice
2 tbsp plain flour	1 tsp vanilla essence
2 tbsp sugar	1 pint milk
cream	orange juice

Take 9 oz boiling water from the kettle and pour into a glass jug. Immediately sprinkle over the gelatine. Stir in juice from the strawberries, and top up with orange juice to make a total of 18 oz in the jug. Stir well.

Break scones into halves so they are full thickness. Pour jelly over the top then put in strawberries so they are evenly distributed. Place in refrigerator to set. In a saucepan, whisk the flour with the milk or favoured milk substitute. Add the remaining milk, sugar, and heat over medium low, stirring constantly till chosen consistency, then stir in vanilla. Allow to cool and pour over set jelly. Whip the cream with 1 tbsp sugar and top the cooled custard.

Friday

Cottage pie

250 g mince	1 small onion, diced
250 g red lentils	mashed potatoes
1 vegetable stock cube	

Cook the lentils in water according to packet directions and drain. Brown the mince. In a casserole dish, mix lentils and mince and diced onion. Sprinkle the stock cube over and mix well. Top with the mashed potatoes and cook in centre of a preheated 200°C oven for 30 minutes, then place under a hot grill for 10 minutes to brown the potatoes. Serve with carrots.

Lemon meringue pie

Base
8-9" pie shell, prebaked (see page 14)

Filling

12 oz sugar	3 egg yolks, slightly beaten
7 oz plain flour	3 tbsp butter (or margarine)
12 oz water	2 oz lemon juice

Heated oven to 200°C. Mix sugar and flour in a saucepan. Gradually stir in water. Stir over medium heat until mixture thickens and boils. Boil for 1 minute. Slowly stir half of hot mixture into slightly beaten egg yolks. Beat into remaining hot mixture. Boil 1 minute, stirring constantly. Remove from heat. Continue stirring until smooth. Blend in butter and lemon juice. Pour hot filling into baked pie shell.

Meringue

3 eggs	6 tbsp sugar

Beat egg whites until frothy and stiff. Gradually beat in sugar until stiff and glossy. Spoon onto pie filling, making soft peaks on the surface. Place in hot oven 8-10 minutes or until meringue gently browns on the peaks. Allow to cool before serving.

Saturday

Sausage & apple pie

1 two crust pie crust (page 14)   1 carrot, diced
1 large potato, peeled and diced   1 tsp cinnamon
3 sausages, frozen   2 apples, peeled & chopped
2 tsp sugar

Preheat oven to 200°C. Boil the potatoes. Line a pie dish with half the dough, slice sausages into thirds, and place around the pie bottom. Sprinkle diced apple, carrots and as much as potato as possible without it getting too full. Mix the cinnamon and sugar in a small bowl and sprinkle over the mixture, then top with remaining pie crust. Cut 4 slits into the pie to vent, and place on a baking tray in centre of oven. Bake for 1 hour.

Save remaining cooked potatoes in an airtight container and use for mash another day. Freeze if desired.

Oatmeal raisin cookies

8 oz butter (or margarine)   10 oz sugar
2 eggs   2 tsp cinnamon
1 tsp vanilla   16 oz self raising flour
24 oz porridge oats   4 oz milk (or milk substitute)
8 oz sultanas

Heat oven to 200°C. Lightly grease baking trays. In a large bowl, cream the butter and sugar then beat in the eggs, one at a time. Stir in the vanilla then the flour and cinnamon till well mixed. Add the porridge oats alternately with the milk and lastly, add the sultanas.

Drop by heaped teaspoons 3in apart onto a baking tray and bake for 10 minutes in the centre of the oven. Use a spatula to remove and allow to cool completely. These will be nice, soft cookies, not hard biscuits.

Week 3

Shopping List

5 eating apples
1 Swede
bag of carrots
courgette
potatoes
mushrooms, 2 punnets or 3 tins
2 parsnips
baby carrots
1 cucumber
peas
green beans
2 sweet potatoes or yams or 1 tin of yams
bell pepper (salad pepper or capsicum)
onions
lettuce
bag of tomatoes

eggs
milk
butter/margarine
mayo
cheddar cheese
orange juice
cranberry juice drink (NOT low sugar one)
whipped cream (optional)

1 tin of pineapple in juice
1 tin of peaches
1 tin pears or 2 fresh pears
1 tin of tomatoes

sausages
mince beef
bacon
package of pork steaks
beef roast (or pork)
2 chickens (or 2 bags mixed parts or breasts)

pasta
long grain rice

dried basil
mixed spice
mixed dried herbs
garlic powder
ground cumin
soy sauce (look for K i k k o m a n)
salad dressing of choice
vegetable oil
chilli powder
Worcester sauce
oregano
black pepper
2 envelopes instant mash
passata
chicken stock cube
ketchup

lemon juice
lime juice
soft brown sugar
evaporated milk
cinnamon
vanilla essence
sugar
porridge oats
cornflour
polenta (cornmeal) or taco shells
self raising flour
plain flour
sweetened condensed milk
raisins or sultanas
unflavoured gelatine
ground nutmeg
icing sugar
chopped nuts

Sunday

Polynesian pot roast

Beef roast (or pork)
2 oz plain flour
3 oz vegetable oil
1 8 oz tin pineapple slices in juice
2 oz Kikkoman soy sauce
3 tbsp lemon juice

2 tbsp soft brown sugar
1 tbsp garlic powder
½ tsp dried basil
2 tbsp cornflour
2 oz cold water

Preheat oven to 220°C. Lightly coat meat with flour. In large roasting tin, brown the meat in the oil in the oven. Drain the pineapple, reserving the juice. Whisk juice, soy sauce, garlic, sugar, and basil together. Arrange the potatoes around the roast and pour the juice mixture over. Cover and cook for 2 hours. During the last 10 minutes, top with pineapple slices. Skim off any excess fat and add enough water with pan drippings to make up 2 cups of liquid, and whisk in the cornflour. Cook on medium low heat until thickened and drizzle over the meat. Serves 6.

> You can cook this in a slow cooker, use drained juices in bottom of the crock for the dripping liquid. Whisk the cornflour in briskly to mix it.

Lime loaf

24 oz self raising flour
12 oz milk (or substitute)
2 oz lime juice

6 oz sugar
1 egg, beaten
3 oz vegetable oil

Topping
2 tbsp sugar

1 tbsp lime juice

Preheat oven to 200°C. In a bowl, combine the flour and sugar, then stir in the egg, milk, and lime juice until just moistened, then pour into a lightly oiled loaf pan. Bake for 1 hour in the very centre of the oven. Let cool slightly, then turn out. While still warm, combine the sugar and lime juice for the topping, and sprinkle over the top of the loaf. Wrap up and store over night at room temperature before serving for best results.

Monday

Cheese topped beef pie

1 single crust pie (see page 14)	250 g mince beef
½ tsp dried oregano	4 oz evaporated milk
good dash of pepper	4 oz ketchup or passata
3 oz porridge oats	2 oz minced onion
3 oz sliced mushrooms	¼ bell pepper, diced
3 oz green peas	1 tsp Worcester sauce
4 oz grated cheddar cheese	

Preheat oven to 220°C and place rack so pie will be in centre of oven. Line a 9in pie plate with the pastry. In a bowl, mix everything except the cheese and Worcester sauce. Place in the pie shell and bake for 35 minutes. Toss the cheese with the Worcester sauce and top the pie with it, baking for another 10 minutes. Remove from oven and allow to stand for 10 minutes before serving

Cucumber salad

lettuce	½ cucumber
2 tomatoes	

Slice the lettuce and cucumber thinly, and dice the tomatoes. Toss together and serve with your favourite dressing. Or try the vinaigrette recipe on page 23.

Monday - continued

Frosted raisin bars

3 oz hard fat (eg. butter)	8 oz soft brown sugar
4 oz water	1 egg
12 oz self raising flour	½ tsp ground cinnamon
¼ tsp ground nutmeg	8 oz raisins (or sultanas)
8 oz icing sugar	1 tbsp butter
1 tbsp milk	¼ tsp vanilla
dash of salt	

Preheat oven to 200°C. Cream the hard fat and the brown sugar, then beat in the water and egg. Add the flour, and spices slowly, beating at low speed if using an electric mixer. Stir in the raisins. Spread in a lightly oiled 12in x 9in x 2in rectangular baking dish and bake for 25 minutes.

Combine the icing sugar, milk, and vanilla with a dash of salt., mixing thoroughly. Spread over slightly cooled cookie bars, allow to completely cool, then cut into bars. Makes a tray of about 40 cookies.

Tuesday

Chicken cacciatore

2 oz plain flour	½ tsp salt
1 2-3 lb chicken, cut up	1 16 oz tin tomatoes
8 oz passata	½ onion, diced
¼ bell pepper, chopped	1 tsp mixed dried herbs
½ tsp garlic powder	3 oz sliced mushrooms

Preheat oven to 220°C. In a plastic bag or large lidded container, combine the flour and salt. Add the chicken pieces a few at time and shake to coat. In a large frying pan, heat a small amount of oil and brown the chicken gently on all sides (brown, don't fully cook!). Remove the chicken and place in a large casserole dish. Cut up the tomatoes and combine with the passata, bell pepper, onion, and spices. Pour over the chicken and bake for 45-50 minutes till the chicken is done at the bone and tender.

Serve over pasta.

Instead of using a whole chicken, you can simply buy a bag of mixed pieces allowing 1-2 pieces per person as desired.

Tuesday - continued

Peach topped coffee cake

2 oz hard fat (eg. butter)   4 oz sugar
1 egg   1 tsp vanilla essence
8 oz self raising flour   ½ tsp cinnamon
1 16 oz tin peaches, drained   4 oz milk

Topping
3 oz plain flour   ¼ tsp cinnamon
2 tbsp hard fat   2 oz firmly packed brown sugar
2 oz nuts, chopped (optional)

Preheat oven to 200°C. Cream the fat and brown sugar together, then beat in the egg and vanilla essence. Mix in remaining ingredients and spread in a lightly greased and floured 9in x9in pan. Cut peach slices in half lengthwise then arrange on top of the batter. Combine the topping ingredients, cutting in the fat, and mix until it resembles fine breadcrumbs, then stir in the nuts (if used). Bake for 30-35 minutes till done. Check if it is done by inserting a clean dry knife in the centre, if it comes out clean, it's ready.

Use the evaporated milk leftover from yesterday if desired, adding no more than 2 oz water to make up.

Wednesday

Easy pork schnitzel

4 pork steaks
2 eggs, beaten
4 oz cheddar cheese, grated
16 oz instant mash potatoes

2 eggs, beaten
2 tbsp water
3 oz vegetable oil

Heat the oil over a medium heat. While the oil is warming, combine the eggs and water. Mix together the dry mash powder and the cheese. Dip each piece of meat in the egg mixture, wetting it well, and then coat in the potato mixture. Dip in the egg for a second coating, and again in the potato. In frying pan on medium heat, brown the steaks till coating is brown and firm, then turn and cook till steaks are done. Drain oil off by placing cooked steaks on a piece of kitchen roll on a plate.

Serve with steamed and lightly buttered green beans and baby carrots.

Apple pie

Pastry for two crust pie (page 14)
5 eating apples
1 tbsp sugar

1 tsp mixed spice
1 tsp lemon juice
2 tbsp butter

Preheat oven to 200°C. Peel the apples and cut off from the core. Place apple chunks in the pastry shell. Sprinkle lemon juice over, then mix sugar and mixed spice together and sprinkle over the apples. Dot all over with the butter, then place pastry top on. Seal edges by pressing with a fork, then cut 4 small slits in top for steam to escape. Brush top with a little milk and sprinkle lightly with sugar. Bake for on a baking tray in the centre of the oven for 20 minutes. Reduce heat setting to 180°C and bake for a further 25 minutes.

Thursday

Tacos

tortillas (see page 13)	½ lettuce, shredded
500 g mince	4 oz cheddar cheese, grated
4 oz water	½ onion, minced
1 tsp salt	1 tsp chilli powder
½ tsp dried oregano	½ tsp garlic powder
¼ tsp ground cumin	½ tsp cornflour
2 tomatoes	

Brown mince, seasoning with all the ingredients except the cheese, lettuce and tomato. Drain with a slotted spoon, and spoon into the taco shells until about ⅓ full. Layer with lettuce, then cheese and finally the chopped tomato.

Cranberry jelly

18 oz cranberry juice drink, (non sweetened variety)
1 envelope plain gelatine

Sprinkle gelatine over 8 oz of the juice and allow to soften for 5-10 minutes. Microwave on high for 1 minute, then stir well to dissolve and mix. Stir in remaining 10 oz of juice. Pour into bowls, and allow to set in the back of the refrigerator (may take up to 2 hours).

Friday

Chicken rice roger

6 chicken pieces
6 oz long grain rice, uncooked
1 onion, minced
4 oz sliced mushrooms
16 oz hot water

flour
¼ cup butter
2 tbsp garlic powder
2 chicken stock cubes
salt and pepper to taste

Preheat oven to 200°C. Combine flour, salt, and pepper on a shallow plate. Roll drumsticks in flour mixture to coat and brown in a little oil in a skillet over medium heat. Meanwhile, place the rice, salt, pepper and onion in a 13in x9in baking dish. Dissolve the chicken stock cube in the hot water and add this and the mushrooms to the dish. Arrange browned chicken drumsticks on top of the rice and dot with butter. Bake for 60-65 minutes until chicken is thoroughly cooked and rice is tender. Serves 6.

Pear salad

2 fresh pears, peeled and halved (or 1 tin pear halves, drained)
4 tsp mayo (eating teaspoon, not measuring one)
4 tbsp cheese, grated

Place one pear half in 4 dishes, top with 1 teaspoon mayo and top with 1 tablespoon grated cheese each. Chill in the refrigerator till ready to eat.

Saturday

Sausage in bacon

6-8 plain sausages   6-8 pieces of bacon
6-8 cheese pieces

Slit sausages so open not quite halfway, and not to the ends. Use a potato peeler to slice the cheese thinly. Then stuff the slivers of cheese into the sausages and wrap in bacon. Grill as normal until fully cooked.

Herbed mashed potatoes
Boil usual number of potatoes. Pour into a mixing bowl, add 1 tbsp butter, 1 tsp garlic, 1 tsp mixed herbs, and 2 oz milk. Use electric mixer to beat.

Mixed roast vegetables
1 tbsp vegetable oil   1 tbsp mixed herbs
1 tbsp garlic powder   ½ bell pepper
½ onion   2 tomatoes, chopped
2 parsnips, peeled and sliced thinly   ½ courgette
2 carrots, peeled and sliced thinly   4 oz Swede, chopped

Whisk oil and herbs together, then coat the vegetables and place in a roasting dish. Roast in preheated oven at 220°C for 35-45 minutes.

Sweet potato pie

1 9in pastry shell (page 14)   4 oz margarine or butter
2 oz orange juice   1 tsp cinnamon
1 tsp vanilla essence   ½ tsp nutmeg
14 oz sweetened condensed milk   2 eggs
2 medium sized sweet potatoes, steamed and peeled

Preheat oven to 200°C. In large mixing bowl, mash the yams and butter together, add remaining ingredients except eggs. Blend until smooth and beat in the eggs. Pour into the pastry shell and bake for 50-55 minutes. Cool and refrigerate. Great on its own or served with a dollop of whipped cream.

Week 4

Shopping List

1 aubergine
carrots
yams or sweet potatoes
potatoes
3 medium bananas
3 medium eating apples
onion
bell pepper
2 oz chopped mushrooms
avocado
celery
carrots
mushrooms

cheese
whipping cream
eggs
milk
butter/margarine
strawberry yoghurt
soured cream
20 oz Philadelphia-type soft cheese
orange juice
apple juice

1 8 oz tin pineapple slices in juice
tin of condensed tomato soup
sweet corn
green beans
20 oz strawberries, fresh, frozen, or tinned
2 tins condensed cream of mushroom soup
9 oz frozen spinach
10 oz okra
4 oz peas

rice
pasta

bacon
chicken pieces
4 fillets white fish
1 chicken
1 kg mince
4 pork chops
leg of lamb

dried rosemary
prepared mustard
paprika
malt vinegar
dried mint
vegetable oil
Worcester sauce
black pepper
oregano
ketchup
dried bay leaves
soy sauce
dried tarragon
garlic powder

rum flavouring
instant custard powder
lemon juice
evaporated milk
4 tins sweetened condensed milk
bar of milk cooking chocolate
dried flaked coconut
pecans (whole or shelled)
almond slivers
spring form baking tin
sugar
lime juice
wholemeal flour
soft brown sugar
plain flour
vanilla essence
glace cherries
walnut halves or pieces
bar of cooking chocolate
apricot jam
self-raising flour
cornflour
2 sachets unflavoured gelatine
porridge oats
raisins or sultanas
candied mixed fruit

Sunday

Roast leg of lamb

1 leg of lamb
vegetable oil

8 potatoes
salt and pepper, to taste

Preheat oven to 220°C. Season the meat and then roast with the potatoes in the oil. Serve with mint sauce and roast aubergine.

Mint sauce

6 oz malt vinegar
2 oz water

2 tbsp sugar
3 tbsp dried mint

Bring vinegar and water to the boil and pour over mint leaves to make an infusion. Allow to step for at least 4 minutes, then stir in sugar. Allow to infuse a further 15 minutes and serve when cool.

Roast aubergine

Wash and slice an aubergine thinly, then lightly brush oil on both sides. Roast for 30 minutes, turning halfway through. Grate some cheese and place on top of the slices, and grill till gently browned, then serve.

German chocolate cake

18 oz self raising flour
12 oz granulated sugar
8 oz soured cream
4 oz cooking milk chocolate, melted

4 large eggs
8 oz butter, softened
4 oz milk
¾ tsp vanilla extract

Grease and flour two 8in square baking pans. In a large bowl, combine all the ingredients. Beat with a mixer at low speed until blended. Increase mixer to high and beat for 2 minutes longer. Spoon batter into prepared pans. Bake in a preheated 200°C oven for about 35 minutes, or until a wooden pick or cake tester inserted in centre comes out clean. Remove to racks to cool completely.

Sunday - continued

Topping

6 oz evaporated milk

4 oz light brown sugar, firmly packed

8 oz pecans, chopped

4 oz butter

3½ oz flaked coconut

In a saucepan over medium heat, bring evaporated milk, brown sugar, and butter to a full boil; remove from heat. Stir in coconut and pecans. Set aside to cool to room temperature.

When cake is cool, place one layer on cake platter; spoon half of the coconut mixture onto the layer. Top with remaining cake layer and top with remaining topping and smooth topping around the sides.

Monday

Chicken in orange sauce

2 oz water

6 oz sugar

2 oz milk (or cream)

4 oz orange juice

chicken pieces, 1-2 per person

Marinate the chicken in the orange juice overnight. Put water and sugar in to a medium-sized frying pan and allow to dissolve, then boil. In an additional pan, warm the milk. Slowly pour the hot milk into the sugar and water. Allow mixture to boil and add orange juice from the chicken. Add chicken, turn down to a simmer and reduce. Once the chicken is done and the sauce has thickened, it is ready to serve with herbed rice and steamed, lightly buttered carrots.

Herbed rice

rice

1 tsp garlic

1 tsp tarragon

1 bay leaf

1 tsp oregano

To make herbed rice, simply add all the ingredients to the water as you cook the rice, and stir. Drain as normal once rice is cooked.

Strawberry charlotte

6 oz butter

6 oz sugar

3 eggs

6 oz self raising flour

1 tsp vanilla essence

Start by mixing all the ingredients for the vanilla sponge well then pour into a cake tin. Bake in centre of preheated 200°C oven for 20 minutes. Allow to cool and cut into fingers.

Continued on page 56

Monday - continued

2 sachets plain gelatine

¼ tsp salt

4 oz water

2 tbsp lemon juice

6 oz sugar

4 eggs, separated

20 oz strawberries

8 oz whipping cream

In a double boiler (or use two cooking pans with one over the other with boiling water in the lower pan), mix gelatine, 2 oz sugar, and salt. Beat the eggs yolks with the water and add the gelatine mixture. Add half the strawberries (if tinned, drain first). Cook over boiling water, stirring constantly till gelatine is dissolved, about 8 minutes. Remove from heat and stir in remaining strawberries and lemon juice. Chill in the refrigerator, stirring occasionally, until the jelly mixture mounds when dropped from a spoon. Take the sponge fingers and split in half lengthways and stand them around the edge of an 8 inch spring form baking tin. Beat egg whites till stiff then beat in the rest of sugar and fold into gelatine mixture. Whip the cream and fold in. Turn into the sponge-lined pan and chill until firm. Turn out carefully and serve.

Tuesday

Pot luck casserole

500 g mince
1 small onion, chopped
8 oz cheddar cheese, grated
1 tin condensed tomato soup
1 tsp prepared mustard

16 oz pasta, cooked
4 oz sweet corn
4 oz green beans
4 oz water

Brown the mince and onion until onion is tender and drain off any fat. Stir in 6 oz cheese and remaining ingredients. Pour into a casserole dish and top with remaining cheese. Bake in preheated 200°C oven for 30 minutes.

Banana split dessert pizza

4 oz soured cream
1 tsp vanilla extract
4 oz butter (or margarine), softened
3 medium bananas, sliced
14 oz sweetened condensed milk
1 oz semi-sweet cooking chocolate
8 oz tin sliced pineapple, drained and halved
glace cherries and additional nuts for decoration

6 tbsp lemon juice
8 oz plain flour
6 oz nuts, chopped
2 oz light brown sugar
1 tbsp butter (or margarine)

Preheat oven to 220°C. Lightly grease a 12in pizza pan or baking sheet; set aside. For filling, in a mixing bowl, combine condensed milk, soured cream, 4 tbsp lemon juice and vanilla and mix well. Chill.

In another mixing bowl, beat the butter and brown sugar until fluffy. Stir in flour and nuts and mix well. Press dough into a circle on prepared pan, forming a rim around edge and prick with a fork. Bake for 10-12 minutes or until golden brown. Cool. Arrange 2 sliced bananas on cooled crust and spoon filling over evenly. Dip remaining banana slices in rest of lemon juice. Arrange on top along with pineapple, cherries and additional nuts. Melt the chocolate with extra butter; drizzle over pizza. Chill thoroughly before serving.

Wednesday

Stuffed chops and yams

8 oz eating apple, diced	3 oz celery, diced
2 oz raisins (or sultanas)	½ tsp paprika
2 tbsp butter (or margarine)	4 thick pork chops
1 tin condensed mushroom soup	4 oz soured cream
2 oz water	2 sweet potatoes

In a saucepan, cook the apple, celery, raisins and half of the paprika in butter until the celery is tender. Trim the fat off the chops, then slit each chop from outer edge towards the bone, making a pocket and stuff with the apple mixture, fastening with skewers. Brown in a frying pan and pour off the fat. Stir in soup, soured cream, water, and remaining paprika, cover and cook over low heat for about an hour until tender, add the sweet potatoes, and heat for a further 10 minutes. Stir gently and serve.

Nesselrode cheesecake

9 oz crushed digestives	½ tsp salt
2 tbsp sugar	6 oz butter, melted

Mix digestives and sugar. Stir into melted butter. Mix well. Press firmly on bottom and sides of 9in pie pan. Chill 1 hour before filling.

Filling

24 oz milk (or milk substitute)	1 tsp rum flavouring
5½ oz instant custard powder	4 oz candied mixed fruit
12 oz Philadelphia-type soft cheese	

Beat cream cheese until softened and gradually add 6 oz milk. Beating until well blended and smooth. Stir in the rest of the milk, rum flavouring and custard powder. Slowly beat for about 1 minute, then fold in the fruit. Spoon into the chilled crust, and chill till firm (about 1 hour).

Thursday

Florentine fish

½ onion, finely chopped
⅛ tsp dried rosemary, crushed
2 oz almond slivers, toasted lightly
4 fillets white fish
9½ oz spinach, cooked and drained
1 tin condensed cream of mushroom soup

4 oz rice, cooked
2 tbsp butter (or margarine)
1 tbsp lemon juice
3 oz water
paprika

Cook the onion and rosemary in butter. Add spinach, rice, almonds, and lemon juice. Heat gently, stirring occasionally. Place 2 oz of the mixture over each fish fillet and roll the fillet. Pin together with a skewer and arrange in a shallow baking dish,. Bake in centre of preheated 200°C oven for 20 minutes. While it cooks, blend soup and water, then pour over the fish and cook for another 15 minutes or until fish is done. Stir the sauce lightly before serving, and sprinkle lightly with paprika. Serve with steamed and lightly buttered carrots on the side.

Glazed apple cream tart

2 oz packed brown sugar
2 oz oats
14 oz condensed milk
4 oz apple juice
1 tsp vanilla essence
2 apples, peeled and sliced thinly
4 oz plus 2 tbsp butter, softened

8 oz plain flour
2 oz walnuts, chopped
16 oz soured cream
2 eggs, beaten
4 oz apricot jam
1 tsp cornflour
5 tsp water

Preheat oven to 200°C. In a mixing bowl, beat the butter and sugar until light and fluffy. Stir in the flour, oats and nuts, press firmly into the bottom of a lightly greased pan. Bake for 15-20 minutes until golden. Mix the condensed milk, soured cream, apple juice, eggs and vanilla. Pour into the crust and bake for a further 30-35 minutes. Melt remaining butter, add the apples and cook until tender. Arrange on top of the tart. In a small pan, combine the jam, water and cornflour and heat, stirring constantly until the mixture thickens. Spoon over the apples and chill thoroughly.

Friday

Brunswick stew

2 slices bacon
1 tbsp garlic powder
3 oz water
dash of black pepper
5 oz sweet corn
6 pieces of chicken, cut into small pieces.

1 small onion, diced
1 tin condensed tomato soup
1 tsp Worcester sauce
10 oz okra
5 oz peas

Place all of the ingredients into your slow cooker and cook on low heat for 8 hours.

Lime cheesecake

7 oz soft cheese
1 ripe pureed avocado
¼ tsp salt
1 crumb crust (as made earlier with digestives on page 58)

14 oz tin condensed milk
4 oz lime juice

In a large bowl, beat cream cheese till fluffy. Gradually beat in condensed milk, then the avocado, lime juice, and salt. Pour into prepared crust, and chill 4 hours until set. Refrigerate any leftovers.

Saturday

BBQ beef burgers

2 oz mushrooms	½ small onion, diced
1 tbsp garlic powder	6 tbsp apricot jam
4 tsp soy sauce	1 tsp dried oregano
500g mince	11 oz ketchup

In a saucepan combine all ingredients or place in a microwave-safe bowl and stir, cover lightly with kitchen roll, and microwave on 70% for 2 minutes, then stir, and heat for 3 more minutes till onion and mushrooms are tender and apricot jam is melted. Form mince into patties and grill under a hot grill for 15 minutes, then turn. Brush with the sauce every 5 minutes and serve on baps with remaining sauce.

Cheesy potato wedges

6 medium potatoes	water
3 oz grated cheddar cheese	3 tbsp oil
½ tsp salt	dash black pepper
½ tsp dried oregano leaves	dash salt

Scrub unpeeled potatoes well. Cut each potato in half lengthwise, then cut into even wedges. Boil potato wedges for 5 minutes in salted water; drain and pat dry. Spread potato wedges in a single layer on a lightly greased baking sheet. Sprinkle with oil, spices and herbs. Bake at 220°C for about 15 minutes. Sprinkle with cheese. Bake for another 10 to 12 minutes or until potatoes are golden brown and cheese is melted

Fruit cocktail

1 tin fruit cocktail	strawberry yoghurt

Serve chilled, with a dollop of sweetened yoghurt. See page 26 for the recipe for fresh fruit cocktail if preferred.

Week 5

Shopping list

potatoes
3 parsnips
11 carrots
Petit pois peas
1 onion
1 small courgette
1 bell pepper
8 oz mushrooms
green beans
2 green tomatoes
1 leek

12 oz cottage cheese
grated parmesan cheese
eggs
milk
12 oz mozzarella cheese
butter
whipping cream
any cheese, 8 oz
8 oz natural yogurt
orange juice
apple juice

1 tin any corned beef
1 tin of cherry pie filling
1 tin any tuna, flaked or chunks
1 tin of strawberries
1 tin of sliced peaches in syrup
1 tin black eyed bean
1 tin sweet corn
1 tin condensed cream of mushroom soup
14 oz tin sweetened condensed milk

long grain rice
pasta

1 whole chicken
1 bag chicken pieces
1 bag mince (any kind)
mixed chicken pieces
sausages

passata, 1 large jar
garlic powder
dried mixed herbs
salt
pepper
chicken stock cubes
beef stock cubes
Worcester sauce
dried parsley
vegetable oil

1 bag self raising flour
1 bag plain flour
baking powder
brown sugar
cinnamon
1 tin evaporated milk
unflavoured gelatine
sugar
cocoa powder
bar of cooking chocolate
vanilla essence
brandy flavouring
raisins (or sultanas)

Sunday

Roast chicken

1 2½-3 kg chicken   vegetable oil
salt and pepper, to taste

Preheat oven to 220°C. Remove the giblets and sprinkle the interior cavity of the chicken lightly with salt and pepper, then place in a roasting tin with the wings tucked down. Rub the chicken well with the oil and season. Place in the centre of oven and cook for 1½ hours. Be certain the juices are running clear. You can use a cooking thermometer. The breast should read 82°C and the thigh, 88°C. Never eat undercooked chicken!

Serve with carrots and potatoes.

Black forest torte

6 oz butter   6 oz sugar
4 oz self raising flour   2 oz cocoa powder
1 tsp brandy flavouring   3 eggs
whipping cream   plain bar cooking chocolate
1 tsp brandy flavouring   2 tsp sugar
1 tin cherry pie filling

Cream butter and sugar together then beat in eggs and 1 tsp brandy flavouring, and then beat in flour and cocoa. Beat till creamy. Pour into 2 lightly greased cake tins and bake in centre of a preheated 200°C oven for 20 minutes.

Allow to cool completely, and then place one cake layer on a plate. Whip the cream, adding 1 tsp brandy flavouring and 2 tsp of sugar. Spread some thinly on top of the layer, and then spoon some of the pie filling sparsely around the edges. Place second layer on top, and cover with whipped topping, and spoon cherry pie filling around the edges. Place any remaining filling in the centre, and grate some of the cooking chocolate all over. Keep in the refrigerator until ready to serve.

Monday

Corned beef burgers

200 g tin corned beef	1 tbsp parsley
1 egg	a little flour
pepper	vegetable oil
dash of Worcester sauce	

Roughly chop the corned beef and mix with the parsley. Beat the egg and mix into corned beef mixture. Add just enough flour to bind. With floured hands divide the mixture into 4. Mould into thick burger shapes. Heat the oil in a large frying pan. Fry the burgers for 3-4 minutes on each side.

Glazed carrots

8 carrots, cut into 2in pieces	2 tbsp butter, diced
2 oz packed brown sugar	pinch of salt
pinch of ground black pepper	

Place carrots in a pot of salted water. Bring water to boil, reduce heat to a high simmer and cook about 20-30 minutes. Do not cook the carrots to a mushy stage! Drain the carrots, reduce the heat to its lowest setting and return the carrots to the pan. Stir in butter, brown sugar, salt and pepper. Cook for about 3-5 minutes, until sugar is bubbly. Serve hot!

Creamy rice pudding

16 oz long grain rice, uncooked	2 egg yolks
2 oz water	½ tsp cinnamon
4 oz raisins or sultanas	2 tsp vanilla essence
14 oz sweetened condensed milk	

Cook rice according to package directions. In a large saucepan, combine the condensed milk, egg yolks, water, and cinnamon. Over a medium heat, cook and stir until the mixture thickens slightly, about 10-15 minutes. Remove from heat and stir in the vanilla, cooked rice, and raisins.

Tuesday

Crockpot lasagne

1 courgette, sliced	1 bell pepper, chopped
1 onion, finely chopped	passata
1 tbsp garlic	½ tbsp mixed dried herbs
1 beef stock cube	1 tsp black pepper
500 g mince, any (eg beef')	12 oz cottage cheese
4 oz mozzarella, grated	2 oz parmesan
1 egg	pasta, any
8 oz mushrooms	4 oz mozzarella, grated for top

Puree the vegetables and passata then add the garlic and mixed herbs. Stir in the stock cube and black pepper. This is the sauce base.

Brown the mince and drain off the fat. Stir the meat into the sauce base. In a separate bowl, mix the cottage cheese, mozzarella, and parmesan with the egg and combine well. Spoon a small amount of the meat sauce into the bottom of the slow cooker. Add two layers of pasta, then a layer of the cheese mixture, and sprinkle some mushrooms on top. Repeat with the meat layer and keep alternating the layers until all are used. Sprinkle the extra mozzarella on top and cook on high for 3 hours, or on low for 6.

Real orange milk jelly

1 sachet gelatine	9 oz orange juice
3 oz sugar	9 oz milk (or milk substitute)

Pour orange juice into a microwave-safe jug and sprinkle the gelatine over to soften, waiting 5 minutes. Stir in sugar and microwave on high for 1 minute, then stir well. Stir in the milk and mix well, and pour into bowls. Refrigerate until set. If you like it "frothy" beat at high speed with a mixer until well mixed and frothy, then quickly pour into the bowls and chill until set. This will often make a two layer type milk jelly, ordinary milk jelly below with a bubbly light jelly mixture on top.

Wednesday

Southern fried chicken

8 pieces of chicken	plain flour
salt	1 tsp dried mixed herbs
1 tsp black pepper	vegetable oil

Using a pastry brush, brush each piece of chicken with vegetable oil. Mix the flour and spices in a bag or lidded container. Place chicken inside and shake well to coat. Place in a shallow baking dish and bake in centre of a preheated 220°C oven for 30 minutes, turning once halfway as it cooks.

Homemade gravy

1 chicken stock cube	8 oz water
1 tbsp plain flour (can use leftovers from making the chicken).	

Whisk flour and water together and heat over low heat, crumbling in the stock cube. Stir as it heats, and cook until desired consistency.

Orange sauced cake

3 oz butter	3 oz sugar
3 oz self raising flour	1 tsp vanilla essence
1 egg	

Cream butter and sugar together then beat in flour and vanilla until well mixed and creamy. Beat in egg. Pour into lightly greased cake tin and bake in centre of preheated 200°C oven for 20 minutes. Allow to cool for 10 minutes, then turn out onto a plate and allow to cool completely.

Topping

2 oz butter	3 oz soft brown sugar
1 egg	6 oz orange juice

In a saucepan, mix the butter, sugar, egg and orange juice together. Cook over a low heat for 10-12 minutes until the sauce is smooth and thickened. Pour over the cake and let cool.

Thursday

Tuna cheese casserole bake

8 oz pasta

1 tin of tuna, drained

4 oz sweet corn

3 oz peas

4 oz cheese, grated

1 tin condensed cream of mushroom soup

Cook the pasta, drain and then combine with the tuna, sweet corn, peas and cheese, reserving 2 oz of the cheese. Place in a lightly buttered casserole dish and top with remaining cheese. Bake in a preheated 200°C oven for 30 minutes.

Strawberry yoghurt whip

1 sachet gelatine

1 tin of strawberries in syrup

apple juice

8 oz natural yoghurt

½ tbsp sugar

Drain syrup into a microwave-safe mixing bowl and sprinkle the gelatine over it. Leave for 5 minutes, then microwave on high for 1 minute. Remove immediately and stir. Add the sugar and stir. Then add enough apple juice to take the mixture to the 14 oz mark. Add in strawberries and yoghurt and beat on high until the mixture is light and fluffy. Pour into individual serving dishes and refrigerate until set, about 2 hours.

Friday

Chicken pot pie

2 oz butter (or margarine)   1 leek, chopped
1½ oz flour   ¼ tsp pepper
1 chicken stock cube   8 oz water
8 oz mixed vegetables   7 oz milk (or more water)
2 pieces of chicken, cut up and off the bone
2 ready-made pie crust (or see page 14)

Heat oven to 220°C. Unfold and lay one crust in pie plate. In a large saucepan, melt butter over medium heat. Add leek and cook about 2 minutes until tender. Stir in flour, and pepper until well blended. It will be thick. Stir in stock cube, water and milk; cook, stirring constantly, until bubbly and thickened. Add chicken and mixed vegetables; remove from heat. Spoon chicken mixture into one crust-lined pan, Top with second crust and seal edges with a fork; cut slits in several places on top crust. Bake for 30-40 minutes or until crust is golden brown. Let stand 5 minutes before serving.

You can make 2 of these at the same time and freeze one for another day

Easy caramel flan

½ cup plus ⅔ cup sugar   3 whole eggs
3 egg yolks   24 oz milk (or milk substitute)
2 tsp vanilla essence

Preheat oven to 350°C. Prepare an ungreased 9in round or square 1½ to 2 quart baking dish. Cook ½ cup of the sugar over medium heat in a heavy medium-sized saucepan, stirring almost constantly with a long-handled wooden spoon, until it is melted. It will turn golden first and then very dark brown. about 5 minutes. (Use extreme caution! Cooked sugar is very hot and can burn the skin if it spatters.) Immediately pour the hot caramel syrup into the baking dish and swirl the pan until it coats the bottom. The caramel will harden at this point and melt again later as the flan bakes.

Friday - continued

Gently but thoroughly whisk together the eggs, egg yolks, and the remaining ⅔ cup sugar in a mixing bowl until smooth. Gradually whisk in the milk and vanilla. Pour this custard mixture into the prepared dish. Create a waterbath by putting the dish into a larger baking pan and filling the larger pan with hot water until it reaches halfway up the sides of the small dish. Bake until a knife inserted two-thirds of the way in to the centre comes out clean, about 35-45 minutes. The centre should still be slightly soft, as the flan will finish cooking after it is removed from the oven. Cool in the water bath, then remove baking dish and refrigerate for at least 1 hour or up to a maximum of 8 hours.

Before serving, run a sharp knife around the edge of the flan to release it. Place a large rimmed serving plate over the baking dish and, using both hands, invert both dishes so that the flan and the liquid sauce un-mould onto the platter. Refrigerate again until serving time.

For a real treat, buy some tinned raspberries as well and spoon over the flan before serving.

Saturday

Sausage scones

16 oz plain flour	sausages
3 tsp baking powder	6 oz milk
1 tsp salt	3 oz butter (or lard)

Preheat oven to 220°C. In a bowl, sift the flour through a sieve and then stir in the baking powder and salt. Cut the fat into tiny pieces and work in with fingers until it resembles bread crumbs. Add milk, stir with a fork until just blended. Transfer the dough to a lightly floured board, and knead gently for 8 to 10 times. Roll out the dough till it is ½in thick and cut with floured scone cutter. Bake on an ungreased sheet for 12 minutes.

Gently fry sausages. Drain on towel and make the gravy, same method as for the chicken gravy on page 33, but using a beef stock cube. Carefully cut each scone in half, place a patty inside and spoon in thickened gravy and place on a plate and serve.

Fried green tomatoes

green tomatoes	salt
flour	vegetable oil

Wash and slice the tomatoes, lightly salt and flour, and shallow fry in a pan until the coating is lightly browned and crispy. Drain on a towel to remove excess grease. If tomatoes are out of season, you can also fry an aubergine this way for a surprising and delicate treat.

This is actually a favourite with children.

Saturday - continued

Peach cobbler

Pastry for 2 crust pie (page 14)   1 tbsp butter
1 16 oz tin of sliced peaches   1 tbsp lemon juice
6 oz sugar   ½ tsp vanilla essence
2 oz plain flour   ¼ tsp cinnamon

Preheat oven to 220°C. Line a pie plate with pastry. Drain peaches well, reserving 4 oz of their syrup. In a saucepan, combine the syrup, flour, and cinnamon, and add the reserved syrup. Cook and stir until the mixture thickens and bubbles. Add the butter, the lemon juice, and vanilla, and then stir in the sliced peaches. Place peach filling into the pastry lined pan. Place the second pastry lid on top, and seal and crimp edges with a fork. Cut 4 vent holes in the top and bake for 15 minutes. Remove the pie from the oven and cover the edges of pastry with foil to prevent edges over browning, then bake for 30 more minutes.

Week 6

Shopping List

1 large eating apple
6 large cooking apples
3 large carrots
2 parsnips
6 onions, medium
bell peppers, 1 red, 1 green
1 small orange
1 rib celery
8 oz mushrooms, fresh, frozen, or tinned
10 potatoes

milk (or milk substitute)
8 eggs
16 oz soured cream
butter

28 oz tinned tomatoes
1 tin tuna
1 tin condensed cream of tomato soup
1 tin condensed mushroom soup
1 tin fruit cocktail
1 jar cranberry sauce
1 tin cherry pie filling
1 tin of pears in juice
1 tin of rhubarb
1 of bag of any frozen peas

500 g stewing beef or mince
500 g mince
sausages
4 pork steaks
1 bag mixed chicken pieces

1 bag of any long grain rice
64 oz any pasta

garlic powder
beef stock cubes
chicken stock cubes

poppy seeds
paprika
vegetable oil
black pepper
Worcester sauce
ketchup, any brand
caraway seeds
mixed dried herbs
soy sauce
chili powder
ground rice
dried thyme
bay leaf
salt

wholemeal bread flour
polenta (cornmeal)
1 bag of self raising flour,
treacle
1 bar plain cooking chocolate
vanilla essence
lime juice
lemon juice
cocoa powder
active dry yeast
cinnamon
gelatine
sugar
tapioca
plain flour
rye flour

1 carton orange juice
1 carton apple juice

Sunday

German beef supper

500 g beef stewing meat, cut into ½in cubes, or mince
1 large eating apple, peeled and shredded

1 large carrot, shredded	½ onion, sliced
4 oz water	1 tbsp garlic powder
1 large beef stock cube	1 bay leaf
⅛ tsp dried thyme	2 tsp ground rice
32 oz pasta, cooked	¼ tsp poppy seed

Slow cooker method
Place all ingredients except poppy seeds and pasta in your slow cooker and stir. Cook on low for 6-8 hours or on high for 5-6. Serve over the pasta which has been lightly tossed with the poppy seeds.

Stove top method
Brown the meat to seal in the juice. Then add the apple, carrot, garlic, stock cubes, bay leaf, and thyme. Cover and simmer on low for 2 hours. Remove the bay leaf, add 2 more ounces cold water, and stir in the ground rice. Cook and stir until thickened (or sub 4 tsp cornflour for the ground rice for stove top cooking). Serve over the hot pasta lightly tossed with the poppy seeds.

Pumpernickel bread

1⅛ cups warm water	1½ cups bread flour
1 cup rye flour	1 cup wholewheat flour
1½ tsp salt	1½ tbsp vegetable oil
⅓ cup treacle	3 tbsp cocoa powder
1½ tbsp caraway seeds	2 tsp active dry yeast

Place all ingredients into your bread maker according to manufacturer's instructions. Select crust type to light. This recipe makes a one and half pound loaf.

Sunday

Apple pie

Pastry for two crust pie (page 14)   6 large cooking apples
6 oz sugar   2 tbsp flour
1 tsp cinnamon   1 tbsp butter

Line a pie plate with the pastry. Peel and pare apples from the core and place in the pastry case. Combine the sugar, flour, cinnamon, and sprinkle over the apples. Dot with the butter, and place top crust over. Cut 4 small slits to allow steam to escape, and seal the edges by pressing down with a fork and trim of ragged edges. Bake in the centre of a preheated 220°C oven for 35 minutes.

Monday

Tuna skillet dinner

3 oz celery, finely diced	9 oz peas, frozen
½ onion, finely diced	4 oz water
2 tbsp soy sauce	4 tsp plain flour
16 oz rice, cooked	5 oz mushrooms
1 tin tuna, flaked or chunks, drained	

In a skillet (a large heavy frying pan), cook celery in a tiny amount of oil until tender. Add the peas and onions and slowly add 3 oz water. Heat to boiling, then cover and simmer on low heat for 8-10 minutes until the peas are tender. Combine the soy sauce, 1 oz water, and flour and add to the vegetables. Cook and stir until thickened and bubbly. Gently stir in the remaining ingredients, and heat through.

Crancherry pie

Pastry for a 2 crust pie (page 14)

1 tin cherry pie filling	16 oz cranberry sauce
2 oz sugar	1 tsp lemon juice
¼ tsp cinnamon	2 tbsp butter
3 tbsp tapioca (does not cook into "frogs' eggs" in this recipe)	

In a bowl, combine all the ingredients except the butter. Let stand for 15 minutes. Preheat oven to 200°C. Line the pie plate with pastry, and fill with the fruit mixture. Dot with butter, place top crust on and seal the edges. Cut 4 slits in top, and wrap edges with foil to prevent over browning. Place on a baking sheet and cook in the centre of the oven for 45 minutes.

Tuesday

Italian sausage casserole

1 red bell pepper, diced	1 green bell pepper, diced
2 onions, sliced	2 tbsp mixed dried herbs
1 tbsp garlic powder	salt and pepper to taste
8 sausages	

3 medium potatoes, diced into 1in pieces
28 oz tinned tomatoes, diced with juice

Brown the sausages and cut into thirds. Combine all ingredients in large covered casserole dish and bake in a 350°C oven for about 1½ hours.

Slow cooker method
Brown the sausages and cut into thirds. Place potatoes on the bottom of the pot and add the rest of the ingredients and then stir. Cook on low for 8 hours or on high for 6 hours.

Chocolate orange cake

16 oz self raising flour	14 oz sugar
5 oz milk (or milk substitute)	4 oz butter (or margarine)
3 oz plain cooking chocolate	3 eggs
6 oz orange juice	1 tsp vanilla
peel of 1 small orange, grated	

Preheat oven to 200°C. Beat the flour, butter, milk, and melted chocolate with an electric mixer for 2 minutes, or by hand. Add egg, orange juice, orange peel and vanilla. Pour batter into two greased, lightly floured tins and bake in centre of the oven for 35 minutes. Cool 15 minutes, then serve with orange sauce as below.

Orange sauce

4 oz orange juice	2 tbsp plain flour
2 tbsp sugar	

Combine all the ingredients in a saucepan and stir over low heat until it is thickened and bubbly. Pour between cake layers and over the top.

Wednesday

Mild Mexican chicken

4 oz plain flour	2 tsp salt
2 tsp paprika	½ tsp black pepper
3 oz mushrooms, sliced	½ tsp garlic powder
½ tsp chilli powder	1 medium onion, diced

5-6 chicken pieces (or 1 small whole chicken, chopped up)
10 oz tin condensed tomato soup

Preheat oven to 200°C. In a plastic bag or lidded plastic tub, combine four salt, paprika and pepper. Add 2-3 pieces of chicken and shake to coat well. Brown the chicken on all sides, and then place in a casserole dish. In a bowl, combine remaining ingredients and pour over. Cover and bake for 45 minutes (if need be, cover with foil). Remove cover and cook for an additional 15-20 minutes until chicken is done.

Slow cooker method
Brown the chicken and place in slow cooker. Add all the other ingredients, stir, and cook on low for 7-8 hours or on high for 4-5 hours.

Cornbread

8 oz polenta (cornmeal)	3 oz self raising flour
1 egg, beaten	8 oz soured milk

Combine dry ingredients; add beaten egg and soured milk, mixing well. Pour into greased, heated 8in or 9in iron skillet (a large heavy frying pan). Bake at 220°C for 20 minutes, or until lightly browned. You can also cook the cornbread using a muffin tray.

> To sour milk, add 1 tbsp lemon juice to the milk and leave to sit in a warm place for 20 minutes.

Thursday

Mock stroganoff

500 g mince   1 onion, diced
1 tbsp garlic powder   3 oz mushrooms
2 tbsp ketchup   2 tsp Worcester sauce
1 tin condensed cream of mushroom soup
8 oz soured cream

Brown beef and onion and stir in the garlic powder. Add the mushrooms, soup, Worcester sauce, soup, and soured cream. Cook and stir till heated through and serve over hot pasta.

If you're dairy intolerant, use salad cream or soya cream substitute with 2 tbsp lemon juice added and allow to sour for 15 minutes or use 8 oz natural yogurt if dieting.

Rhubarb crumble

1 tin of rhubarb   4 oz self raising flour
1 oz sugar   2 oz butter

Preheat oven to 175°C. Mix together the sugar and the flour. Then cut the butter into pea-sized lumps and rub in with your hands until the mixture looks very lumpy and crumbly. Drain the rhubarb and place into a baking dish. Spoon the crumble topping mix on to the top. Bake in the centre of the preheated oven for 35 minutes. Serve with custard if desired, see page 31 for the recipe.

Friday

Pork steaks, potatoes, carrots and parsnips

4 pork steaks	8 potatoes
2 carrots	2 parsnips
salt and pepper, to taste	

Peel the vegetables. Then quarter the potatoes, slice the carrots and parsnips. Parboil and then place in a casserole dish. Lightly salt and pepper the pork steaks and place on top of the mixed vegetables. Add just enough water to cover the potatoes. Bake in preheated 220°C oven for 35-45 minutes, until meat is done and vegetables are cooked.

Slow cooker method
Peel the vegetables and then quarter the potatoes and dice the carrots and parsnips. Place the potatoes then carrots and parsnips in the bottom of the pot and add just enough water to cover the potatoes. Place lightly salted and peppered pork steaks on top of the vegetables. Cook on high 6-7 hours or low for 8 hours.

Pear jelly

1 tin pears, in juice	4oz apple juice
1 packet plain gelatine	1 tbsp sugar

Stew the pears in just enough apple juice to cover and then strain juice into a jug. Dice the pears. Sprinkle the gelatine over juice and allow to soften. Add the sugar, and microwave on high for 1 minute, then stir well. Add more juice (use some from the tinned pears) to make liquid up to 18 oz, and mix in diced pears. Pour into bowls and allow to set, about 2 hours.

Saturday

Crockpot chicken 'n' dumplings

4 pieces chicken, cut into small pieces
1 chicken stock cube   4 oz peas
1 tbsp mixed dried herbs

Place the chicken in pot of your slow cooker and cover with water.
Crumble in the stock cube and then add the peas. Cook on high for 3-4
hours or on low for up to 6-7 hours. During the last hour, add the
dumplings.

Dumplings
6 oz self raising flour   3 tbsp butter
3 oz milk or water   ½ tsp black pepper

Mix all the ingredients together except the black pepper. When blended,
add pepper. Dough should be very stiff, just workable. Drop dough into the
broth in the slow cooker by heaping tablespoonfuls. Cook for a further 30
minutes.

Key lime pie

1 pie crust, baked (see page 14)
12 oz sugar   6 oz plain flour
¼ tsp salt   20 oz water
4 eggs, separated   3 tbsp butter
4 oz lime juice   4 oz sugar

Separate the eggs while cold, putting whites into a large bowl. These
should be kept at room temperature for meringue. Put the yolks in a small
bowl and beat lightly, set aside. In a heavy saucepan stir together the sugar,
flour and salt. Slowly stir in water until smooth and then bring to the boil,
stirring constantly. Reduce heat and let the mixture bubble for
approximately 8 minutes, stirring all the while. Remove from heat. Stir

Saturday - continued

several spoonfuls into the yolks, mixing thoroughly, and then add this to the rest of the mixture in the saucepan. Stir over medium heat for 5 minutes. Remove from heat. Stir in the butter and lime juice, mix until smooth. Cool thoroughly at room temperature. Spread over the crust, making certain it touches edges of crust at all points. To make the meringue, beat the egg whites until foamy. Slowly add ½ cup sugar, 1 tbsp at a time, beating at high speed until the meringue forms firm peaks. Spread the meringue over the filling, making sure it also touches the edges of the crust. Bake at 200°C for 12 minutes or until lightly brown.

Allow to cool and don't cut the pie for 2-3 hours.

Week 7

Shopping list

1 bell pepper (any colour)
5 small onions
potatoes
1 head white cabbage
1 large carrot
bean sprouts
1 stalk of celery
2 ripe bananas
8 oz fresh mushrooms
5 plum tomatoes
1 courgette

1 dozen eggs
1 large container natural yogurt
8 oz soured cream or plain natural yogurt
3 8 oz packages soft cheese (cream cheese)
butter/margarine/lard for baking
4 oz mature cheddar cheese
½ pint whipping cream

1 tin condensed cream of mushroom soup
4 tins of sliced mushrooms
1 tin of baby carrots
2 ¼ oz tinned ripe olives
2 tins of tomatoes
1 tin of tinned pork (such as pek)
2 tins of tuna
1 large tin of sweetened condensed milk
2 tins of gooseberries
1 tin crushed pineapple
1 tin of rhubarb
1 tin raspberries
1 tin strawberries

1 bottle 7UP® or other lemon-lime pop

ice lolly molds

1 bag long grain rice
1 packet cogliche pasta
1 packet of spaghetti

vegetable stock cubes
1 envelope onion soup mix
red lentils
1 bag plain flour
2 jars passata
dried mixed herbs
yeast
vegetable oil
soy sauce
BBQ sauce
vinegar
1 package plain digestives
1 package sponge fingers
1 bar plain cooking chocolate
lemon juice
allspice
ginger
cinnamon
sugar
vanilla essence
soft brown sugar
chopped walnuts
white chocolate chips
gelatine

250 g lamb mince
3 chicken pieces
6 slices streaky bacon
1½-2 kg beef roast
750 g mince
1 package of sliced pepperoni
diced pork

Sunday

Pot roast

1 beef roast   1 envelope onion soup mix
1 tin condensed cream of mushroom soup

Place all the ingredients in a lidded roasting tin and cook on 180°C for 1½ -2 hours, or until meat checks as done.

Slow cooker method
Place roast in crockpot and pour over the condensed soup. Sprinkle over the dry onion soup mix, and cook on low for 8 hours.

No bake chocolate raspberry cheese cake

2 oz butter, melted   10 oz digestive crumbs
1 envelope unflavoured gelatine   2 oz sugar
4 oz plain cooking chocolate, melted 16 oz cream cheese
14 oz sweetened condensed milk   1 tsp vanilla essence
½ pint whipping cream   1 tin of raspberries

Whip the cream and set aside in the refrigerator. Combine the melted butter, digestive crumbs, and sugar. Press firmly onto the bottom of a 9in springform pan (or pie plate). In a microwave-safe jug, place 5 oz of the syrup from the raspberries and sprinkle the gelatine over it. Allow to stand for 2 minutes and stir, then heat on high in the microwave for 1 minute. Remove and stir well. Set aside.

In a large mixing bowl, beat the cream cheese and melted chocolate until fluffy. Gradually beat in the condensed milk and the vanilla and mix till smooth. Slowly beat in the gelatine mixture and fold in the whipped cream. Pour into the prepared crust. Drain the remaining raspberries well and spoon over the cheesecake. Chill for 3 hours.

Monday

Shepherd's pie

250 g lamb mince   1 small onion, diced
250 g red lentils   mashed potatoes
1 vegetable stock cube

Cook the lentils in water according to packet directions and drain. Brown
the mince. Then, in a casserole dish, mix the lentils with the mince and
diced onion. Sprinkle the stock cube over and mix well. Top with the
mashed potatoes and cook in centre of a preheated 200°C oven for 30
minutes, then place under a hot grill for 10 minutes to brown the potatoes.

Serve with baby carrots.

Gooseberry pie

two pie crusts (page 14)   2 16 oz tins gooseberries
6 oz sugar   2 oz plain flour
1 tbsp butter (or margarine)   small pinch of salt

Preheat oven to 220°C. Drain the gooseberries. Combine sugar, flour, and
salt in a mixing bowl, mixing well. Add the sugar mixture to berries;
tossing gently to coat the fruit. Fill a pastry-lined 9in pie plate with the
berry mixture; dot with butter. Place top crust on, seal and flute the edges.
Cover edges of the pie with aluminium foil.

Bake in the centre of the oven for 20 minutes. Remove foil and bake for
25 minutes longer or till golden but not browned. Cool on a wire rack or
trivet.

Serves 8.

Tuesday

Pepperoni pizza

¼ cup warm water (40°C)
½ cup room temperature water
16 oz plain flour
1 tbsp sugar
4 oz mature cheddar cheese
2 tbsp mixed dried herbs

1⅛ tsp dry yeast
3 tbsp vegetable oil
1½ tsp salt
pepperoni
1 green bell pepper, diced
passata

Preheat oven to 200°C. Put the warm water into a small mixing bowl. Sprinkle the yeast over the water and let stand until the yeast softens, about 3-5 minutes. Mix slightly to dissolve the yeast, stir in the sugar, and allow it to proof for another 15 minutes in a warm spot in the kitchen. Add the room temperature water and 1 tbsp of the olive oil to the yeast mixture and stir to combine.

Measure the flour and the salt into the bowl of a stand mixer, or place in a food processor. Combine on very low speed with the paddle attachment. Slowly add the liquid ingredients to the dry and increase the speed of the mixer slightly to incorporate. Stop the mixer and replace the paddle with a dough hook, if you have one. Knead until the dough becomes smooth and begins to pull away from the sides of the bowl, about 4 minutes. Place the dough on a floured board and knead by hand for another 1-2 minutes. Add flour to dust as needed to prevent sticking.

Shape the dough into a ball and place in a very lightly oiled bowl and cover with a clean towel. Let stand until dough doubles in size, about 1 hour. When the dough has doubled in bulk, divide it into 6 equal pieces (about 6 oz each). Set the pieces of dough required on a sheet pan and cover with a clean towel or plastic wrap. Dough not being used can be placed in the refrigerator or frozen until ready to use.

On a lightly floured surface, roll each piece of dough as evenly as possible into a 10 inch circle, dusting lightly with flour as necessary. Use fingers to create an edge and paint middle with passata. Grate the cheese and

Tuesday - continued

sprinkle half of it over the base, and top with the pepperoni and the diced green pepper. Sprinkle a generous couple of pinches of mixed dried herbs over the top and then add the remaining cheese. Place in centre of oven and bake until golden brown, about 10 minutes.

If you have a bread maker, make the dough by adding the ingredients for in the order your manufacturer suggests and then use the dough setting. Then follow the recipe for the topping as above.

Frozen strawberry yoghurt

1 container natural yoghurt   1 tin strawberries in syrup
1 tsp vanilla essence

In a large mixing bowl or liquidiser, combine the yoghurt, strawberries in syrup and vanilla essence. Mix until pureed smooth and pour into ice lolly molds or other serving dishes and freeze until set.

Wednesday

Spring rolls

Filo pastry (see page 12)

250 g mince	1 large carrot, finely diced
1 teacup (not mug!) bean sprouts	1 stalk of celery, sliced thinly
2 teacups white cabbage, shredded	2 tbsp soy sauce
½ tsp allspice	¼ tsp ginger
¼ tsp cinnamon	salt and pepper, to taste

2 tbsp plain flour mixed with 3 tbsp water

Blanch the carrots, bean sprouts, celery and cabbage in boiling water until soft, drain and set aside. Heat oil in a wok or frying pan and add the mince and stir fry until cooked, add the vegetables, and combine well. Add the soy sauce and spices, the salt and pepper and the flour paste. Stir thoroughly and place to one side to cool. Remove pastry from plastic bag, covering with a damp cloth to keep it from drying. Peel off pastry sheets as required.

Place pastry with a corner facing you, so it looks like a diamond. If you're making large spring rolls use 6 oz of filling, if making mini spring rolls use 1 tbsp of filling. Centre the filling (so it looks like a sausage) on the pastry about 3in above the bottom corner. Lift the bottom corner over the filling and roll once. Fold the sides over and continue to roll.Seal the exposed corner of the pastry with cornflour paste to prevent the roll from opening.

Heat the vegetable oil in a saucepan or deep fryer. When the oil is hot enough (170°C), add the spring rolls and cook until the pastry is golden. Cooking time is approximately 5 minutes for a large spring roll and 3 minutes for a mini roll. Drain spring rolls on absorbent paper. Serve with soy or sweet chilli sauce.

Put unused pastry into a plastic bag and store in the freezer. You can also make extra spring rolls in advance and freeze for another day.

Wednesday - continued

Chicken a la King

1 tin mushrooms, sliced	2 oz butter
2 oz plain flour	½ tsp salt
16 oz milk (or milk substitute)	½ tsp pepper

3 chicken pieces, skin removed and meat taken from bone.
2 tbsp onions, very finely chopped

Melt the butter in a saucepan and saute the drained mushrooms. Blend in flour and salt and stir until bubbly. Add milk and cook, stirring constantly until sauce boils and thickens. Add chicken, onion, and pepper. Heat through. Remove from heat and serve over rice.

Pineapple pudding

3 eggs	8 oz sugar
small pinch of salt	4 tbsp plain flour
16 oz milk (or milk substitute)	1 tsp vanilla essence
1 tin crushed pineapple	sponge trifle fingers
½ pint whipping cream	

In a saucepan, mix the eggs and sugar, beating well. Stir in the salt, flour and milk. Bring to a boil over medium-high heat, stirring constantly and cooking until thickened. Remove from heat and let cool for 2 minutes, then stir in the vanilla. Drain the crushed pineapple well, and break up the trifle fingers.

In a serving bowl, layer some of the trifle fingers, then some of the pineapple, then some of the custard and repeat till finished, reserving a tiny amount of crushed pineapple. Whip the cream and dollop on top to garnish, sprinkling the reserved crushed pineapple over the cream.

Thursday

BBQ pork

500 g pork, diced	½ tsp black pepper
1 onion, finely chopped	1 bottle bbq sauce

Slow cooker method
Place diced pork and onion into the slow cooker and pour over ¾ of the bottle of the bbq sauce, giving it a good stir. Cook on low for 5-6 hours. Serve with baked beans and German potato salad.

German potato salad

6 streaky bacon slices, cut into ½in pieces

1 small onion, chopped	6 oz vinegar
2 tbsp sugar	¼ tsp pepper

5-6 cups potatoes, cooked and sliced

In frying pan, fry the streaky bacon over medium low heat until crisp. (Do not preheat skillet). Pour away all but 2 oz of the bacon drippings and add the onion, vinegar, sugar and pepper. Cook and stir over low heat, uncovered until mixture simmers. Place potato slices in a bowl, pour liquid over and toss lightly to combine. Season to taste with salt. Garnish with crumbled bacon slices. Makes 6 to 8 servings

Banana rhubarb fool

1 tin rhubarb	2 oz soft brown sugar
1 tbsp sugar	1 tsp ground ginger
8 oz cream cheese	2 kg bananas, thinly sliced

Drain and puree the rhubarb, sugar, ginger and most of the banana. Save half a banana for decorating, leaving in the skin to prevent browning. Mix well and gradually beat in the cream cheese. Place in serving bowls and decorate with remaining banana just before serving.

Friday

Pasta salad

16 oz cogliche pasta

1 4 oz vegetable oil

1 tsp garlic

½ tbsp dried oregano leaves

1 large courgette, chopped

1 tin (2¼ oz) sliced ripe black olives, drained

5 plum tomatoes, coarsely chopped

8 oz passata

2 oz vinegar

2 tsp dried basil leaves

8 oz fresh mushrooms, sliced

1 medium onion, chopped

Cook and drain pasta as directed on package. Rinse with cold water an drain. Mix passata, vinegar, vegetable oil, garlic, basil and oregano in a large bowl. Add remaining ingredients; toss. Cover and refrigerate about 2 hours or until chilled then serve. Keep no longer than 48 hours.

Blonde brownies

4 oz butter, room temperature

1 egg

pinch salt

8 oz white chocolate chips

8 oz soft brown sugar, packed

8 oz self raising flour

7 oz walnuts, chopped

Cream together the butter and brown sugar; beat in egg. Stir in the flour and salt. Next stir in the nuts and the white chocolate chips. Spread batter in a greased and floured 7in x 11in pan. Bake at 200°C for 20-25 minutes.

These brown very quickly, so be sure to start checking right at the 20 minute mark

Saturday

Tuna bolognaise

1 tin tuna	1 jar passata
1 tbsp garlic powder	1 tbsp dried mixed herbs
1 tin of tomatoes, diced	8 oz fresh mushrooms
1 level tbsp sugar	

Place all of the ingredients in a large pan and simmer together for 20 minutes over low heat. If you're making this in a slow cooker, put all of the ingredients in the pot, stir and cook on low for 4 hours. Serve over spaghetti.

The sugar in this recipe takes away the acid and tempers the flavour.

7UP® cake

12 oz butter, softened	24 oz sugar
5 eggs	24 oz flour
2 tbsp lemon flavouring	icing sugar
6 oz 7UP® (or other lemon-lime beverage)	

Preheat oven to 200°C. Cream butter and sugar until smooth. Add eggs, one at a time, beating well after each addition. Add flour, lemon flavouring and 7UP® and mix well. Pour into greased cake pan. Bake in centre of the oven for 1 hour 15 minutes or until done. Sprinkle with icing sugar.

Don't use a diet drink or one with artificial sweetners as this makes the cake bitter.

Week 8

Shopping List

1 bag of potatoes
1 rib of celery
1 orange
green beans
4 carrots
1 green bell pepper
2 sweet potatoes
2 large onions
2 small onions

butter or margarine
1 container natural yogurt
milk
single cream
2 dozen eggs
3 oz Gruyere cheese (deli counter)
8 oz salami (deli counter)
soured cream or natural yogurt
mild cheddar cheese
cream cheese
orange juice

2 tins of condensed cream of mushroom soup
2 tins condensed cream of chicken soup
1 tin condensed cream of tomato soup
1 tin of mushrooms
1 tin apricot halves
1 tin cherry pie filling
1 tin evaporated milk

ribbon noodles
long grain rice

1 lb fresh coley fish
500 g mince
4 pork steaks
bacon pieces
6 chicken pieces
diced beef (or beef flank steak, diced)

Worcester sauce
dried parsley
mixed dried herbs
chicken stock cube
tomato puree
salt
black pepper
garlic powder
prepared mustard
vegetable oil

soft brown sugar
sugar
nutmeg
cinnamon
1 large bag of icing sugar
glace cherries
chocolate chips
self raising flour
plain flour
dried currants
vanilla essence
ground cloves
dried coconut
baking powder
porridge oats
1 bag of pecans
2 bars plain cooking chocolate

frozen peas

Sunday

Chicken stroganoff

6 chicken pieces, meat cut from the bone
4 oz plain flour   1½ teaspoons salt
½ medium onion, finely chopped   ⅛ teaspoon pepper
16 oz hot water   1 chicken stock cube
1 tin sliced mushrooms   3 tbsp tomato puree
6 oz soured cream (or plain natural yoghurt)
1 tsp Worcestershire sauce

Coat chicken strips evenly with a mixture of flour, salt, and pepper. Heat a
small amount of vegetable oil in a heavy frying pan and add the chicken
and onion; brown evenly on all sides. Add hot water and stock cube, cover,
and simmer about 20 minutes or until meat is tender. Add mushrooms to
the chicken. Remove skillet from heat. Combine sour cream, tomato puree,
and Worcestershire sauce. Add in small amounts to the meat in skillet,
mixing well. Return to heat and stir over low heat until hot. Serve over
hot, buttered noodles.

Chocolate refrigerator cookies

4 oz butter (or margarine)   8 oz sugar
1 egg   ½ tsp vanilla essence
10 oz self raising flour   1 tsp baking powder
2 oz plain cooking chocolate, melted 3 oz pecans, finely chopped

In large mixing bowl blend the butter and melted chocolate. Mix in sugar,
egg and vanilla. Blend flour and baking powder, then add slowly to the
sugar and egg mixture. Divide dough into two equal parts. Shape each part
into a roll 1½in in diameter and about 7in long. Roll in pecans to coat,
pressing lightly. Wrap in plastic wrap; refrigerate for at least 2 hours.
Preheat oven to 220°C. Cut rolls into ¼ in slices. Place slices 1in apart on
ungreased baking sheet. Bake for 8-10 minutes, or until just set let sit for 5
minutes then remove to rack to cool completely.

Monday

Beef burgundy

500 g diced beef, cubes cut in half
2 tbsp butter (or margarine)   1 large onion, diced finely
1 tbsp dried parsley   ⅛ tsp black pepper
1 tin condensed cream of mushroom soup
2 oz red wine (cheapest plonk is fine)

In a frying pan, gently brown the meat in the butter. Add the other
ingredients, stir, and cover. Simmer over low heat for 1 hour or until
tender, stirring occasionally. Serve over noodles.

Slow cooker method
Brown meat and put all ingredients into the crockpot, giving it a good stir.
Cook on low for 4-5 hours.

Carrot cake

2 eggs   4 medium carrots, peeled
8 oz self raising flour   ½ tsp cinnamon
4 oz butter (or margarine)   2 oz pecans, chopped

Preheat oven to 180°C. Shred or grate the carrots. In a mixing bowl, mix the
flour, cinnamon, butter and eggs. Stir in the carrots till moistened then beat
well (two minutes on medium speed if using electric mixer). Spread evenly
into a greased and floured baking tin and bake for 35 minutes.

Cream cheese frosting
3 oz cream cheese   3 oz butter (or margarine)
1 tsp vanilla essence   20 oz icing sugar
3-4 tsp milk (or milk substitute)   dash of salt
handful of chopped pecans

In mixing bowl, beat cream cheese, butter, vanilla essence and salt. Slowly
stir in icing sugar and mix well. Add milk until it's of spreading consistency.
Use to frost cooled cake and sprinkle chopped pecans over the top.

Tuesday

Pork a l'orange

4 pork steaks	black pepper
8 oz orange juice	¼ tsp ground cloves
2 tins condensed cream of chicken soup	
½ long rib of celery, sliced diagonally	
8 slices of fresh orange, cut in half (not orange sections)	

Cut off any fat from the pork steaks. Brown the steaks, pour off any fat and season lightly with black pepper. Stir in remaining ingredients except the orange slices. Cover and simmer on low heat for 40 minutes, stirring occasionally. Add the orange slices and cook over low heat a further 5 minutes.

Slow cooker method
Remove fat from steaks and season with black pepper. Place in crockpot with all ingredients except orange slices and give a good stir. Cook on low 4-5 hours and in last 15 minutes, arrange orange slices on top.

Herbed rice

rice	water
2 tsp mixed dried herbs	1 tsp dried parsley

Measure out the water and the rice and add mixed dried herbs and parsley to the cooking water. Serve lightly tossed with butter or margarine or with the gravy from the pork steaks.

Tuesday - continued

Oatmeal crème pies

8 oz butter (or margarine)
1 tbsp vanilla essence
12 oz self raising flour
12 oz soft brown sugar, firmly packed

6 oz granulated sugar
4 egg whites
24 oz porridge oats

Heat oven to 200°C. Combine butter, brown sugar, sugar and vanilla in large bowl. Beat at medium speed of electric mixer until well blended. Beat in egg whites. Add flour gradually to creamed mixture at low speed. Beat until well blended. Stir in oats with spoon. Mix until well blended. Drop by rounded tablespoonfuls 2in apart onto ungreased baking sheet, flattening lightly. Bake 8-9 minutes or until light brown. Cool on baking sheet about 30 seconds before removing to cooling rack. Cool completely.

Frosting

16 oz icing sugar
½ tsp vanilla extract

2 oz butter (or margarine)
milk (or milk substitute)

Combine the icing sugar, butter and vanilla in a medium bowl. Beat at low speed, adding enough milk for good spreading consistency. Spread on bottoms of half the cookies. Top with remaining cookies.

Store in an airtight container.

Wednesday

Cheese and salami pie

single pie crust (see page 14)   1 small onion, diced finely
1 tbsp flour   dash of black pepper
8 oz evaporated milk (or soya)   8 oz (weighed) salami
2 oz (weighed) mild cheddar cheese, grated
1 large potato, peeled, diced, and boiled

Preheat oven to 220°C and arrange rack so the pie will be in centre of the oven. Line a pie plate with the pastry and prick the bottom with a fork. Bake it for 10 minutes and remove from the oven. Reduce the oven temperature to 200°C. Then in a saucepan, whisk together the milk and flour and a dash of black pepper. Cook over medium low heat, stirring consistently, till bubbly and thickened. Remove from heat and stir in the grated cheese till the cheese has melted. Add the salami and onion and pour into the pie shell. Bake on a baking sheet for 35 minutes and allow to stand 5 minutes before serving.

Cherry-ocolate cake

1 oz (weighed) plain chocolate   16 oz self raising flour
8 oz sugar   6 oz milk (or milk substitute)
4 oz butter (or margarine)   2 eggs
1 tin cherry pie filling

Remove 6 tbsp of the pie filling and set aside in a separate bowl. Preheat oven to 200°C. Melt the chocolate and set it aside. Combine flour and sugar in a large mixer bowl. Make a well in centre then add milk, butter, cherry pie filling and eggs. Blend at low speed until moistened. Beat for 2 minutes at medium speed. Add melted chocolate and beat until well mixed. Pour into a greased and floured 13in x 9in x 2in pan. Bake for 25-30 minutes or until a knife inserted in centre comes out clean. Allow to cool in the pan completely. Top with the cherry chocolate sauce (recipe can be found on the next page).

Wednesday - continued

Cherry chocolate sauce

1 oz plain chocolate
16 oz icing sugar

2 oz butter (or margarine)
6 tbsp cherry pie filling

Melt the chocolate and butter in a saucepan. Beat in the icing sugar alternately with cherry pie filling saved from the cake recipe until smooth.

To serve, turn out the cake onto a plate, and top with the sauce, then cut cake into squares.

Thursday

Spanish rice with beef

500 g mince	1 small onion, diced
½ green bell pepper	2 tsp garlic powder
8 oz water	4 oz rice, uncooked
2 tsp Worcester sauce	generous dash black pepper
1 tin condensed cream of tomato soup	

In a frying pan brown the meat and cook onion and bell pepper till soft. Drain the fat, and add the remaining ingredients. Bring to the boil, then cover and lower heat to low. Cook for a further 25-30 minutes on the simmer or until rice is tender.

Spiced currant bars

8 oz butter (or margarine)	6 oz sugar
6 oz soft brown sugar, packed	2 eggs
3 oz orange juice	24 oz self raising flour
½ tsp cinnamon	¼ tsp ground cloves
12 oz dried currants	10 oz dried flaked coconut

Preheat oven to 200°C. Melt the butter then stir in both types of sugar. Add the eggs, beating the mixture well after each one. Blend in the orange juice, then stir in the flour and spices. Fold in the currants and coconut. Spread evenly into a greased and floured rectangular pan. Bake for 20 minutes, then allow to cool thoroughly and frost with orange icing.

Orange icing

12 oz icing sugar	3 tbsp orange juice
1 tbsp butter, melted	

In a bowl, beat icing sugar with orange juice and butter, until smooth and spread over the bars.

Friday

Bacon quiche

Pastry for single crust pie (see page 14)
½ small onion, diced   4 oz Gruyere cheese, grated
3 eggs, beaten   1 tsp prepared mustard
8 oz single cream (or soya)   dash of ground nutmeg
6 pieces bacon, cooked till crispy and crumbled

Preheat oven to 220°C. Line pie dish with pastry and flute the edges. Don't prick the pastry. Place silver foil over the pastry, pressing gently into place and use dried beans to hold it down. Bake for 15-18 minutes until the edges are lightly browned. Allow to cool for about 10 minutes, then gently remove the beans and the foil. Reduce oven temperature to 180°C. Cook the onion in vegetable oil till softened. Sprinkle the cheese into the bottom of the pastry shell and top with the crumbled bacon, then onion. Whisk together the remaining ingredients and pour over the cheese, bacon, and onion. Bake for 40-45 minutes until set and allow to stand 10 minutes before serving.

Sweet potato cupcakes

6 oz (weighed) self raising flour   pinch of nutmeg
6 oz (weighed) butter (or margarine) 6 oz (weighed) sugar
2 eggs   2 tsp cinnamon
2 sweet potatoes, boiled, peeled, and mashed

Preheat oven to 180°C. Grease or line a muffin tray. Combine all of the ingredients in a large bowl; beat on medium speed for 3 minutes. Pour batter into prepared cups, filling ¾ full and add topping below. Bake for 25-30 minutes or until a knife inserted in centre comes out clean. Cool in pans on wire racks for 10 minutes; remove to wire racks to cool.

Topping
4 oz cream cheese, softened   1 large egg
2 tbsp sugar   5 oz chocolate chips

Beat cream cheese, egg and sugar in a small bowl until smooth. Stir in chocolate chips. Spoon about 1 tbsp of topping over batter.

Saturday

Fisherman's pie

1 lb coley	3 oz peas

4 large potatoes, mashed with butter
1 tbsp dried parsley
1 tin condensed cream of mushroom soup

Place coley on a microwave-safe plate and cook on high for 4 minutes. Remove fish and allow to cool. Flake fish with a fork and place in bottom of a casserole dish and sprinkle the peas over. Then spoon the condensed soup over the other ingredients. Top with the mashed potato and sprinkle with the dried parsley.

Bake for 20 minutes in preheated 220°C oven then brown under a hot grill for 15 minutes or until potato is browned.

Apricot salad

1 tin apricot halves, drained	4 tbsp natural plain yoghurt
2 tbsp icing sugar	4 glace cherries

Place apricot halves in serving dishes. Mix the yoghurt and sugar to sweeten and place one tablespoon on centre of each apricot half. Top each one with a glace cherry.

Index